J. Edgar Thomson

THE GEORGIA RAIL ROAD YEARS, 1833 – 1845

J. Edgar Thomson

THE GEORGIA RAIL ROAD YEARS, 1833 – 1845

F. Lewis Smith

Deeds Publishing | Atlanta

Copyright © 2017 — F. Lewis Smith

ALL RIGHTS RESERVED—No part of this book may be reproduced in any form or by any electronic or mechanical means, including information storage and retrieval systems, without permission in writing from the authors, except by a reviewer who may quote brief passages in a review.

Published by Deeds Publishing in Atlanta, GA
www.deedspublishing.com

Printed in The United States of America

Layout design by Mark Babcock & Matt King
Cover design by Mark Babcock

Library of Congress Cataloging-in-Publications data is available upon request.

ISBN 978-1-944193-92-8
EISBN 978-1-944193-93-5

Books are available in quantity for promotional or premium use. For information, email info@deedspublishing.com.

First Edition, 2017

1 2 3 4 5 6 7 8 9 0

It is my pleasure to dedicate this book to
two of the finest Christian men I've ever known:

Robert E. Knox, Jr. and B. DeWayne Patrick, Lt. Gen. (ret)

Their contributions to the communities of Thomson and Augusta, Georgia are, and have been, too valuable to be calculated. Their leadership within the civic, political and military arenas of the state of Georgia has been a model of respect, dignity and honor which we should all follow.

Contents

Preface   xi

1. Early Stagecoach Travel and Thomson's First Glimpse Of Augusta   1
2. Early Georgia Rail Road and Blacks in Augusta   13
3. Lombardy, Raw Whiskey and Weekend Fights   27
4. Cap' Wilson, Frogpond, and Wrightsboro   41
5. The Fox-Hunt at Foxboro   51
6. Making Progress, Settlers, and Squatters   61
7. Fruitland, Corporate Slavery, and The Financial Panic Of 1837   75

Photographs   87

8. Money Problems and The Yellow Fever Epidemic   103
9. Insider Dealings, Railroad Barons, Augusta Take-Over, and Gold   111
10. Dahlonega Gold and The Trail Of Tears   123
11. Spanish Cruelty, The Five Civilized Tribes, and Indian Practices   129
12. Relocate Terminus, Sherman, Slavery,
    Impending Doom, and Bloody Tariffs   139
13. Early Passenger Travel, The Marietta Party, and The Augusta Canal   153
14. Goodbye Georgia Rail Road and Hello Pennsylvania Rail Road   167

Epilogue   177
Acknowledgments   181
Bibliography   183
About the Author   185

Preface

The life and times of John Edgar Thomson can be separated into two distinct time periods. It's very easy to study the latter period, his days building and nurturing his beloved Pennsylvania Railroad. The years when Edgar Thomson held the company's reins are called the Pennsylvania Railroad's "Golden Years."

But I challenge you to find one hundred pages written about the first period, the beginning of his life and his twelve years as a professional engineer of the Georgia Rail Road. You will have to remember as you read this book that the actual name of the railway was the Georgia Rail Road, until its name was changed in 1836 to the Georgia Railroad and Banking Company.

I was born and raised in Augusta, Georgia, but I have lived in nearby Thomson for thirty-five years. As the Director of the McDuffie Museum, I often read about Edgar Thomson. I developed a great desire to dig into the history of this most illustrious railroad tycoon and industrialist of his time. Because so few people know much about Edgar Thomson's great Georgia story, I wanted to change that. But I wanted to tell his story in an enjoyable atmosphere; I wanted you, the reader, to see that history can be fun and educational at the same time.

James Ward, the author of the definitive biography of Thomson, included only two chapters totaling forty-three pages about Thomson's

Georgia years. Forrest Beckum and Albert Langley's book the *Georgia Railroad Album* has many fantastic pictures of the road's locomotives and depots, but it has only two pages of the railroad's history. These two books contain forty-five of the one hundred pages I mentioned.

In 1975, the first nineteen honorees selected to *Fortune Magazine's* National Business Hall of Fame included John Edgar Thomson. Some other selectees you may recognize were Henry Ford, Thomas Edison, and J. P. Morgan. The great Cornelius Vanderbilt did not make the first cut. Thomson was praised by the selection committee for developing the most innovative methods for railroad construction in the industry to that time. He was an advocate and consumer of the newest technological advances of the world.

Thomson also originated the departmental system of organization of corporate management still in use today. This was the system of separating the functions of a business into sales, administration, personnel, maintenance, etc. Thomson received the greatest praise from the selection committee not because of his abundant wealth, which was minor compared to many of the other selectees, but because, as they declared, "no scandal touched this man."

I have used James A. Ward's *J. Edgar Thomson, Master of the Pennsylvania* as the timeline and the meat for this historical novel. Mr. Ward's biography of Thomson was chosen in 1980 as the 33rd volume to be issued in *Contributions in Economics and Economic History*. Mr. Ward's twenty-six page story in the 1976 issue of *Railroad History No. 134* titled "J. Edgar Thomson and the Georgia Railroad 1834—1847" was culled by him virtually word-for-word from his *Master of the Pennsylvania* biography, so I haven't counted those pages again.

Mary G. Cumming's *Georgia Railroad & Banking Company 1833—1945* relives the early history of this first railroad in Georgia. She spent many months reading the worn and dusty pages of the bank's minutes of stockholders' and directors' meetings until they became vivid and vital to her. She read old diaries and letters and newspaper clippings to weave her story into the living thing she had tried to create. Her story has contributed to my book as much as James Ward's has. I have taken what history I could from Mr. Ward and Mrs. Cumming and other sources and added to them what I thought were interesting tidbits and histories of the towns and taverns along the railroad route Thomson laid from Augusta to Atlanta.

Another source I have used to tell two true stories in this book came from *Georgia Scenes* which originated from the pen of Augustus Baldwin Longstreet. In the early 1830s, as he wrote them, stories from Longstreet's *Georgia Scenes* appeared in Georgia newspapers. He then had the Augusta Steam Press Company publish them in book form in 1835. The stories I've condensed here are "The Fight" and "The Fox-Hunt." The fight actually took place in Lombardy, now present day Dearing, Georgia, and the fox-hunt actually occurred near Wrightsboro, Georgia. Both were seen, remembered, and recorded by Longstreet in the 1830s and were as true as his memory would allow.

The descriptions and stories of the black folks in Springfield came from the Edward J. Cashin history, *Old Springfield: Race and Religion in Augusta, Georgia*. Springfield had been a separate village until 1798 when it was incorporated into Augusta. Cashin tells the honest tale of the way life was lived there and its people.

Another book of Augusta history written by Dr. Cashin is *The Story of Augusta*, a 1980 Richmond County Board of Education textbook. I had hoped it would be chock full of Georgia Railroad history, but I was surprised. Dr. Cashin's book has plenty of information about Augusta, particularly in the 1820s through the 1850s. Unfortunately, reading through the two chapters covering 1818 through 1860, I found only a word or two about Thomson and his railroad.

Maybe Dr. Cashin couldn't find any readily available information about them and didn't think they were worthy of deep research. Maybe he tried, but gave up. He said that U. S. histories generally focus on New England, and that's because New Englanders wanted to make their history known, so they wrote about it.

Usually, people think Georgia history is only about Savannah in the earliest days or about Atlanta in the later days. By learning her history, Augustans and their neighbors can judge Augusta and her surrounding cities against the rest of Georgia and its Georgians.

I'll admit it is a queer combination to intertwine textbooks from the 1940s and the 1980s and a local history from the 1990s with the first book of humorous realism in American literature from the 1830s. While supplying its readers with valuable information about Thomson and the Georgia Rail Road, Ward's textbook was unfortunately limited in its scope due to a lack of information available on Thomson during his early years.

Mr. Ward had "become convinced that J. Edgar Thomson did not want anyone to write his biography" due to the virtual impossibility of obtaining any material about him. Ward should know; he spent a decade searching for it. Mr. Ward said that Thomson seldom saved any of his personal correspondence, and most of that little bit of material was lost by water damage fifty years after his death. Ward obviously relied to a great extent on Mary Cummings' book for his own book, but Ward also wrote his work by using the letters he found in other people's correspondence with Thomson. Using others' letters unfortunately provides only one side of the story, doesn't it? That is not Mr. Ward's fault.

I would like to point out that as you are reading this, you'll see many references to $4,000 a year or $5,000 a year or $3,369,000 in construction costs. I want you to be aware that the normal salary for the average working man in America during this time from 1834 through 1846 was around $300 a year. Today's average personal salary would equal about one hundred times what it was then. Please keep that $300 a year figure in mind. It was the average salary of a man, not just in the unindustrialized South, but also in the big-time business world of the North.

I'd say that, at a minimum, ninety-five percent of this book is factual. I had only to structure Thomson's non-existent conversations so that the facts could be told. I say non-existent because Thomson was not the chatter-box I've portrayed him as here. He was quiet and reticent and hardly spoke at all. He was not a person who attended gala events and balls. He did plenty of charity work but it was by using his dollars, not his time or personal input.

Even the words spoken by William T. Sherman about the upcoming belligerence between the States are true; I took them from an actual letter he wrote. However, the letter was written in the late 1850s, not the middle 1840s, but that was my largest stretch. As to Mr. Sherman's personal views about events of the day, I know he didn't care a lick about Indians or slaves.

Did Sherman actually say the other things as I have written here while at the White Ladies' Ball? He could have. He was a Lieutenant stationed at the Augusta Arsenal in 1844 and Edgar Thomson was a captain of industry in Augusta in 1844. Why couldn't the two men have met? They may have shared their feelings about slavery, which are true as presented here. Of course, the Ball would have been at one of Augusta's elite's mansions, or at the Medical College, and not at the Arsenal. I had to put it there so the lowly Lieutenant Sherman could attend without a formal invitation.

Was there a White Ladies' Ball? Certainly. At that time people could say white or black, or acknowledge that there were some differences between the two, without worrying whether someone was going to have a heart attack about it. There was, at that time, and there is still, an almost family bond of affection between white and black people who lived and worked with each other peacefully in most parts of the South.

Did Thomson ever meet Dennis Redmond? Or Cap' Wilson? Did he ever visit Wrightsboro? Did he know Epp Wilson? No one knows, but he may have. However, I do believe that he could not have missed experiencing the richness and excitement of the black culture of Springfield.

Because of those questions and more, this is an historical novel, not a pure history book. But the essence of the events are factual and speak to that time in history. I only had to stretch a few dates and locations to make a little of the information presented here compatible as to time and place. At times, just for fun, I've used the actual names of persons I know. I hope no one is offended.

This is the story of J. Edgar Thomson's Georgia Rail Road and Banking years, 1833-1846, and little snippets of the history of the towns and people from Augusta to Atlanta at that time. I hope you enjoy it. And please take this with you: In the author's opinion, Edgar Thomson contributed more to the success of early Georgia and the Georgia Railroad than any other person.

1 Early Stagecoach Travel and Thomson's First Glimpse Of Augusta

Young Mr. Thomson was surprised when he stepped from the railroad platform of the *Best Friend of Charleston* in Hamburg, and saw that not just one, but eight, stagecoaches were ready to transport him to Augusta, his final destination. When a baggage handler asked him if his trip had been agreeable, Thomson replied, "The trip to this point has been relatively pleasant, thank you. The only true irritant I've suffered so far has been the misplacing of my surveying equipment. It wasn't your company's fault. The steamship crew in New York left it on their dock." Upon his arrival in Charleston the previous day, Thomson discovered the error. It tore his nerves to pieces, but he was assured the transit was safe and was promised a delivery date in Augusta in about three weeks. He just had to wait it out, but patience wasn't his strong suit.

"Most of my equipment was top quality, though really just standard pieces, but I was very concerned over the possible loss of my favorite transit." Thomson and his friend William Young, an instrument maker from Thomson's hometown of Philadelphia, had developed a special transit which was to become the standard surveying instrument of the nineteenth century.

Thomson was privileged, he thought, to travel on the Charleston and Hamburg Rail Road. As a railroad man, he was impressed that he could see firsthand the operations of the longest railroad in the world under one management. The South Carolina Canal and Rail Road Company built the railroad primarily to capture the cotton trade that was leaving upstate and western South Carolina. The majority of that cotton had been shipped by wagon to Georgia, which proved to be a closer, more convenient method of getting the cotton to England. That was, until the Charleston and Hamburg was completed in 1833.

Passengers paid eight dollars to travel the railroad's 136 miles of track from Charleston to Hamburg. Leaving Charleston at 7:00 a.m. every morning, the train pulled up in Hamburg, later known as North Augusta, at 4:00 that afternoon. The trip was pleasant, flat, uneventful, and quick.

The Charleston and Hamburg Railroad had just been completed. There had been no thoughts on building a railroad bridge over the Savannah River to Augusta. It would be many years before that marvel would be accomplished. Frequent floods on the river flowing between Hamburg and Augusta often uprooted massive trees, sending them cascading downstream. Without fail, these trunks caught on anything sticking out of the water, including bridges. As soon as two or three trees snagged on a bridge or its pilings, the pressure on the wooden structures caused them to give, bringing the whole bridge down into the water.

No one could afford the expense of building a new bridge in the same spot every two or three years. These were usually privately constructed, and fees were charged to patrons who wished to cross over the bridge. Only on state roads were government funds available to pay for the enormous costs of building and maintaining new bridges.

The entire trip on the rails from Charleston to Hamburg had taken nine hours, and Thomson looked forward to crossing the Savannah River into Georgia to begin the most exciting journey of his life. The afternoon sun shone bright as he purchased his ticket for the short stagecoach trip. This time, not depending on some hot, tired, underpaid hireling to handle it, he thoroughly checked his luggage and equipment himself.

The stagecoaches prepared to load their passengers; there had been forty-six aboard the train from Charleston. "My good man, what's the pecking order here for boarding these coaches? I'm headed for Augusta. I am tired and anxious to go. Which one is mine?"

The conductor looked at Thomson's ticket. "That is your coach, sir, there. As soon as each coach is ready for boarding, we encourage passengers to climb inside. Going to Augusta? You could board the Augusta stage or the Macon stage. They both stop in Augusta. Have a good trip, sir. Augusta is quite a town. She should be; she was a hundred years old two years ago."

When a coach was full, it would leave for its destination. Some passengers were getting off in Augusta, like Mr. Thomson, while others were continuing to Macon for further connections there to all points west. Not all coaches were crossing the river; some were taking their passengers north to upper South Carolina, and some were headed along the long dark river for Savannah and Hilton Head (changed to Port Royal during the Civil War and now back to Hilton Head).

Once the coaches had arrived in Augusta, there were three main dirt roads they could use to leave the city. One road took passengers and cargo to Washington via Washington Road. Travel to the northeast Georgia mountains and upstate South Carolina also took Washington Road. Another road took similar traffic, passengers and cargo, to Wrightsboro via Wrightsboro Road. At Thomson, it forked toward Barnett and Warrenton.

The third stage road squeezed between the other two and passed through Scott's Ferry. No major roads led to Savannah because most traffic floated down the Savannah River to it. Why take a slow, dirty, crowded stagecoach trip when a fast, clean, peaceful boat ride was available?

Some of the coach drivers were black, some white. There were four horses to each coach, and all the horses were ready, harnessed, and excited. The passengers were getting off the train and into the coaches, and their luggage was being transferred in noisy wheelbarrows. The horses became frightened and impatient to start. The black drivers were talking to them in loud, wild voices; the white drivers were hollering as if they were already at mid-trip, going fifty miles an hour.

Thomson had settled into his seat. "Good day, sir," said the well-dressed lady next to him.

"Good day, madam, how are you? Hope you're enjoying your trip."

"I am, sir, but I am a little wearied and I worry how these coaches will ride," she said.

Thomson had wondered about that, too. "These coaches look like fine European coaches, madam, but they aren't that good. I travelled throughout Europe a few years ago, mainly by coach. I have noticed that instead of flexible springs, these American coaches are hung on straps of what seem to be leather. They don't flex and I hope they don't break! It doesn't seem to matter which coach you choose, they are all the same. Look how they're covered with mud from the roof to the wheel-tire. They apparently have never been washed since they were built."

The coaches had only one step, and it was almost a yard from the ground. The step was usually reachable through the use of a chair. It wasn't the easiest thing to do, this boarding the stagecoach. Thomson had complained as he got on board, "How in this world do ladies get on this thing?"

The attendant leaned in and whispered to him, "We help the ladies climb up on the chair and onto the step. However, if there are lady passengers, but no chair handy, the unfortunate creatures depend on a pull from the inside. Or, worse, a push or two from the rear."

The coaches held nine inside, having three rows of seats from side to side. The only thing worse than getting into one of the infernal contraptions was getting back out again. There was only one outside passenger, and he sat on top. This was always a man, because no lady or even a common woman would ever take that seat.

Thomson's driver was a black man. He was very black and Thomson had never seen such a thing. His face almost glowed; it reminded Thomson of an enormous piece of polished coal, or maybe a large, beautiful eggplant. He was dressed in a coarse suit excessively patched and darned, especially at the knees. He had on grey stockings, huge wallowed out shoes, never touched by blacking, and very short trousers. He had two odd gloves, one of worsted, and one of leather. He had a very short whip, broken in the middle and bandaged up with string. He wore a low-crowned, broad-brimmed, black hat, faintly giving forth an insane image of an English coachman.

The coachman, when finally assured that all passengers had taken their places, yelled "Go ahead!" at the top of his lungs, and the four anxious horses roared to life. The short, two-mile trip to Augusta was over a bridge built twenty years earlier by Henry Shultz.

Shultz, an industrious man from Hamburg, Germany, wanted his small community of Hamburg, South Carolina, to economically surpass and punish the competing metropolis of Augusta. He had been wronged by the Georgians and wanted blood. The Augustans had used their political pull to keep their state from granting a charter to Shultz which would have allowed him to build a railroad bridge from Hamburg to Augusta. It was strictly a business move; Augusta merchants did not want any competition upsetting the existing tolls for using their toll bridges.

The driver rolled his eyes and screwed up his face as if he believed this could be his last voyage over the river. Fortunately for Mr. Thomson, the uneventful trip ended at the hitching post as scheduled, on November 1, 1834, in front of the Augusta Mercantile building on Broad Street.

Honoring prior arrangements made by Mr. Thomson's new associates, Thomson was shown to his room at Mrs. Hall's delightful boarding house opposite the U. S. Post Office on Broad Street. Young Thomson signed the house's register as "J. Edgar Thomson, Professional Engineer, Philadelphia, Pennsylvania." He was met there by the men he had hired in advance of his arrival: an assistant, two rod-men, two chain bearers, and two axe-men.

The weather was kind, and the large clock outside the Post Office promised a little over two more hours of sunlight when Thomson ventured onto the sidewalks of Augusta's main street for the first time. The sidewalks were crowded with women and young girls who likewise had come out to see what was of that day's interest in town, but in their case, they wanted also to be seen. They twirled their fashionable parasols, which they used to protect their delicate white skin as they pranced around.

Augusta was a handsome city of 6,530 persons, but was very regular in shape due to its being laid out parallel to the Savannah River. As Edgar walked around for an hour or so, he began to wish that there was a crooked street to walk, just for a change of pace. He visited the various public institutions on Broad Street. Here he found an excellent hospital, a quaint old library, the Mercantile Exchange and the Post Office. Taverns and eating salons were in abundance and some patrons sat on the sidewalks.

Thomson hopped into a bookstore. Looking around, he spoke to the man who seemed to be the proprietor, "I say, you certainly seem to have quite an inventory. I am a little surprised, I didn't realize there would be so many readers down here. But now that I've interrupted you, may I ask you a question? Why were all these streets laid out so straight?"

"Certainly, I am glad to be of service to you. The town was laid out in 1736 by General James Oglethorpe in the same forty-lot square pattern he had used for Savannah. Nothing has been changed to that plan these ninety-something years. I think it makes the town look nice and neat."

Augusta indeed showed its splendor. There were magnificent homes and beautiful parks all through the city. Everything in town appeared to be in motion. The very streets seemed to be starting up of their own accord, ready-made, and looking as fresh as new, as if they had been turned out of their workmen's hands just an hour before.

Just five years earlier, in 1829, the heart of Augusta had been devastated by a horrific fire. Almost every building from a block above to two blocks below Centre Street and from Broad Street to Greene Street were turned to ashes. Almost five hundred buildings were lost, including a new theater, a new marketplace, and a new hospital.

Arson was suspected and to guard against another episode the streets were filled with armed volunteers under Colonel William Cumming. Mayor Samuel Hale headed a community meeting which solicited funds for the victims' relief. The hotels which had escaped the inferno opened their doors to the homeless. They were the United States, the City, the Planters, and the Eagle Tavern. Henry Shultz offered his vacant houses across the river in Hamburg to the needy.

Some houses were still half painted, while the foundations of others, within just five yards' distance, were only beginning. Many churches, courthouses, jails, and hotels were in view on Broad Street and on the side streets. Several of the side streets further from the center of town were nearly finished but had not yet received their names. Many others were in the opposite situation, being named but not having been started. Their location was signified only by a line of stakes.

Here and there Edgar was pleased to see the proof that a grand city was forming along the river. There were great warehouses, without window sashes, but half filled with goods and furnished with cranes, ready to fish up the huge pyramids of flour barrels, bales, and boxes lying in the streets.

The town boasted a beautiful Government House and a fine new Academy of Richmond County. In the center of town, the spire of a Presbyterian church rose to a great height, and on each side of the supporting tower was to be seen the dial-plate of a clock. The city was alive.

The growth of Augusta westward beyond the city limits had reached Harrisburg by the 1790s. An important tobacco merchant, Ezekiel Harris, had built a magnificent home on a hill there. The surrounding citizenry named the hamlet Harrisburg in his honor. Harrisburg church-goers were also very proud of their new Presbyterian Church.

Mr. Harris had been quite successful in South Carolina as a tobacco merchant, and moved his business to Augusta. In 1794, he bought 323 1/2 acres west of Augusta to develop a tobacco trading center. His goal was to rival the Augusta market.

Harris built a large tobacco warehouse on the Savannah River for acquiring, storing, selling, and disbursing tobacco leaves. He constructed his large house in 1797 to accommodate planters who arrived with their crops. He established a free ferry across the river to entice business to his warehouse.

Unfortunately, Harris was not a very good businessman. He began selling off lots for residential development in 1799 due to some large and costly lawsuits. The proceeds from their sales could not stem the tide for him financially. The area surrounding his home became known as the Village of Harrisburg in 1800.

At about the same time and not but a couple of miles from the Ezekiel Harris House, George Walton built his beautiful home, Meadow Garden. Walton had moved to Augusta after the Revolution when it had been named the state capital in 1786. Although many outstanding early government leaders also made Augusta their home, Walton was the most influential. He was a signer of the Declaration of Independence, a Georgia governor, a United States Senator, and a judge on the state Superior Court.

The Augusta area had played a significant role during the American Revolution. While the war was almost at a stalemate in the North, it was still being fought with passion in the South. The British could not stop the patriotic citizens of the region from continuing the war. In honor of the men who contributed so much to the cause for freedom, Augusta had named its main streets for important Revolutionary War generals. The town had always been flush with patriotic fervor and showed it in an amazing way. Washington Street was named for General George Washington, McIntosh Street for General Lachlan McIntosh, Jackson Street for General James Jackson, Elbert for General Samuel Elbert, Lincoln for General Benjamin Lincoln, and Greene Street for General Nathanael Greene.

These half-finished, whole-finished and beginnings of streets were crowded with people, carts, stages, cattle, and pigs, far beyond the reach of numbers. As all these were lifting up their voices together in a grand chorus, the clatter of hammers, the ringing of axes, and the creaking of machinery added to make a fine concert.

After this quick perusal of the center of town, Thomson immediately began a new walk. He couldn't wait to study Augusta's outer countryside. To himself he asked, *"Where will be the best place to locate my depot? Where shall we place our line?"* But it would be dark soon, and he had just a little time. He had to hurry; he had no intention of getting lost in the dark in a new city.

On the train from Charleston, Thomson had constantly moved about, changing seats time and again, disturbing the other passengers. "I apologize sincerely, madam, I am so excited over my new job. I cannot wait to get my transit in my hands and begin my work. I can't sit still."

"That's okay, young fellow, we Southerners understand that you Northerners can't keep still, even for a moment. Down here we applaud your intensity of purpose in getting a job done as quickly and as efficiently as possible. But remember, son, that intensity is exactly the thing that most of us Southerners find so annoying in Yankees. Apparently y'all can never be still, always having to do something. Good luck with your new railroad, young man; I hope it's a success." That intensity would become the defining aspect of Edgar Thomson's life.

Throughout his life, Thomson lacked an obsession with the love of money and the absolute devotion to greed that most of his contemporary railroad cronies had developed. Although he spent his entire life in the pursuit of profit, in keeping with his Quaker background, he used, in absolute contrast to his more flamboyant contemporaries, only a tiny amount of his future income for personal pursuits.

Every morning, as Edgar waited in Augusta for his transit to come, he would piddle in his new office downtown. He had it furnished and organized in no time. Often he walked to a favorite small café a block from the city's enormous waterfront along the river. One morning, hearing the sound of voices raised in song, he edged to the river and came upon eight black laborers engaged in unloading a barge's cargo. One of the laborers struck up a chantey, and all the movements of the men kept time with the music. It was a monotonous chant, which rose or fell according to whether the load was heavy or light. He watched and listened for a while, enthralled at the magic of the moment.

At his table, he asked his waiter, "How long have the Negroes been singing at the wharf? Are they special or do all the slaves sing while they work?"

"Well, Mr. Thomson, the black men and women down here make a habit of singing while they work. I hear tell that during their first months of captivity the wretched slaves will fall into a terrible state of melancholy. They become deaf to their masters' calls and even indifferent to their blows. The only thing that will arouse the slaves is their music, and they force themselves to sing to keep their spirits up. Besides, it reminds everybody of their suffering and so maybe it's a good thing they sing."

A hundred years earlier, before General Oglethorpe and his Georgia trustees, the entire countryside in the area that became Augusta was covered with a dark silent forest. No one could proceed in any direction without coming completely against the woods of time immemorial.

When the white man intruded upon that forest, it was eventually cleared for cultivation. The stumps were left standing for many years because it was easier, as well as more profitable in other respects, to plough around them. The profit was found in not wasting the time and labor in rooting them out, or burning them up, or blowing them up with gunpowder.

But when the forest that became Augusta was levelled with a view to building a town in its place, a different system was, of course, used. The trees were removed immediately or a little later, according to the owner or to the circumstances of the case. One Augustan who had enough capital would clear his lot to the woods, and erect his house or shop across it. But, on his neighbor's land the trees would still be growing. Edgar could see that on the far outskirts of town, stumps of trees were in the roadway, causing travelers to dodge them at their peril.

J. EDGAR THOMSON, THE GEORGIA RAIL ROAD YEARS, 1833 – 1845

One morning, after his breakfast, as Edgar walked to the town's limits, as such, even though its only indication was its lack of any development, he came upon a man, alone on the unfinished road. The man was standing in a space about an acre in size, roughly enclosed, on a gentle swell of land. Even though reluctant to speak to a stranger out here, Edgar couldn't help but ask, "What can this strange place so far from town be, my good man?"

"Oh, this is a graveyard, sir. You know, a burying-ground. Most of the local people are buried here. You may not be from around here, but in Georgia we don't usually use churchyards to bury our dead, if that's your question."

2 Early Georgia Rail Road and Blacks in Augusta

*As much as Edgar was enjoying his education into the lives of the sophis-*ticated and the common folks of Georgia, he was dying to get his surveying equipment and to get to the job at hand. He had, after all, been hired by the Georgia Rail Road Company to build a commercial railroad or possibly a turnpike road for stagecoaches and wagons. The road would run from the city of Augusta, with branches extending to the towns of Eatonton, Madison, and Athens, and to places farther west when the company finally decided in what direction it would go.

In June, 1833, a meeting was held in Athens to consider the promotion of a railroad to improve the transportation of goods into central Georgia. The meeting's chairman was Asbury Hull. It was he who introduced the bill for the incorporation of the Georgia Rail Road.

A public meeting was held in Augusta on July 20, 1833, just sixteen days after arrival of the first train from Charleston to Hamburg. The meeting was called by Mayor Samuel Hale, W. W. Montgomery, James McLane, William Gould, and John P. King to consider building a railroad from Augusta to Athens.

Given that authority by the legislature of the state of Georgia in December of 1833, a group of prominent businessmen from Athens met in the library of James Camak's house on March 10, 1834, to accept the state charter and to select directors of the new company. For his hospitality in hosting the meeting, Camak was elected the company's first President. William Williams was elected Secretary and Treasurer. The first members of the company's Board of Directors were James Camak, William Dearing, William Williams, James Shannon, William Cunningham, E. L. Newton, Alexander B. Linton, John Nesbitt, William Lumpkin, Henry B. Thompson, John A. Cobb, Absalom James, and John Cunningham.

The Act passed by the Georgia legislature contained a provision that the company had to have 5,000 shares of common stock with a $100 par value per share subscribed within three months. Subscribed means that someone had to pledge or guarantee that they would purchase those shares for cash at a later date when the Board determined the money was needed for operations.

The charter by the state to allow the company to build its stagecoach or railroad line would be void if the company couldn't quickly raise the $500,000 in pledges. That was no problem; the stock was totally subscribed in that first meeting. Another noteworthy accomplishment was that the City Council and the Trustees of the Academy of Richmond County had conveyed to the railroad ten acres of land on the Town Commons. On January 1, 1835, maps were presented to the Board of Directors showing the railroad's route and its termination at the lots conveyed to the company.

Director William Dearing of Washington, Georgia, was sent to New York City to negotiate a first mortgage loan on the road and to have a corporate seal made for the company. Two months later, Dearing was back with the disappointing news, "Gentlemen, there are no northern bankers who are interested in loaning money on an unsurveyed road with no definite route. It does seem ludicrous to me now upon further reflection that we could have even hoped one would."

James Camak added, "Sirs, I am unwilling at this point to admit defeat. We have too much time and money in this endeavor to quit now. I move that the Board continue diligently with our project. My first choice in engaging a professional to do our location work is the Army Corps of

Engineers. They are experienced, but more importantly, they are free. The Corps has helped everyone with as many of these projects as they could. Maybe they can squeeze us in. I particularly want us to engage Colonel Stephen Long. I've corresponded with him and I think he is the man we need. He's the best engineer in the country. Unfortunately, he says he cannot come until after he has located a road in Memphis. He has no idea when he'll be finished, so we need to find someone else."

In August, 1834, the Board asked director William Williams for a special favor. Camak said, "We want you to go up North to examine the railroads up there so that we can learn from their mistakes. Take notes and ask questions of as many knowledgeable people as you shall meet. Be on the lookout for a competent chief engineer. That engineer would be responsible to locate our lines, construct our tracks and superstructure, and equip our railroad. That will be a significant job with tremendous responsibilities. If you happen to find such a man, employ him at once before he changes his mind or someone else tinkers with him." According to the company's minutes, Mr. Williams was allowed for this service three dollars a day and reasonable expenses.

The directors sent Williams up North because they felt no one was available in the South at that time who could handle the job. They weren't prejudiced; they just wanted someone who could get along with them, with southern contractors and southern laborers, someone who knew the peculiar institution of the South. In October, Williams returned to Athens with a contract in hand between the Georgia Rail Road Company and J. Edgar Thompson, as it was incorrectly spelled. There was no "p" in this Thomson, but that error would continue for the rest of Edgar's life.

How could Williams travel over 1,000 miles to Philadelphia and so quickly find a man of twenty-six who was capable of assuming the important position of chief engineer unless he had been recommended by a trusted associate? He couldn't have. William Hassell Wilson had recommended Thomson for the position, although indirectly, through his mutual professional contacts in Georgia and South Carolina.

Charleston-born and highly educated, Hassell Wilson and his much respected father located the rail line for the Philadelphia and Columbia Railroad in 1828. He was later to become, in 1859, the resident engineer of the entire Pennsylvania Railroad. Being from Charleston, Wilson had kept up with the affairs of the Charleston & Hamburg Railroad. He had previously recommended Thomson to those Charleston folks when he thought young Thomson was ready to expand his career.

When William Williams passed through Charleston on his way to Philadelphia, he paid a business call on the C & H executives. At that meeting they mentioned Wilson's high praise for his old protégé, Edgar Thomson. On a personal level, Edgar had corresponded regularly with three of his prior railroad associates who were engineers on the Monroe Railroad connecting Macon to Forsyth. These men may have also recommended Thomson to the Georgia Rail Road directors.

Although he left Athens without a clue as to whom or what to find, the shortness of William Williams' trip to Philadelphia, after such praise, indicates he went there to find Thomson. The fact that the twenty-six year old Thomson accepted a $3,000 per year salary, at a time when the average American worker was making around $300 a year, shows how highly regarded Thomson was. In comparison, the entire railroad labor force during the summer of 1835, eight months after Thomson's hiring, were white men, working for the princely sum of fourteen dollars a month and board.

As irritating as it was not to have his equipment, its absence did give Thomson the time to introduce himself to the company's Board in Athens. He took the stagecoach through Wrightsboro and on to Washington and finally to Athens. He was boarded on this special trip at the home of James Camak, the company's first president. William Williams had resigned as Treasurer on October 27, 1834, and James Camak had been elected to fill the offices of both President and Treasurer for $2,500 a year, plus $500 for expenses.

No Board member except Williams had seen Thomson, but they were all pleasantly surprised by his appearance and his demeanor. "Welcome to

Athens, Mr. Thomson, and welcome to the South. On behalf of the Board of Directors of the Georgia Rail Road let me say that we are all very glad to have you as a partner in this great undertaking upon which we have so recently embarked. Please tell us a little about yourself."

"Thank you. I'm happy to accommodate you gentlemen. I normally would say in short order that I am from Delaware County, Pennsylvania, and that I learned my trade beside my father. I have no formal training as an engineer, as I told Mr. Williams. But because I now work for the Board and the company, I feel that I should tell you the rest of the story of how I got here.

"Before my birth my father was a farmer, but he had a great mechanical mind. He naturally leaned towards settling personal boundary disputes and platting unsettled parts of Pennsylvania. He championed better transportation methods around the state and constructed possibly the country's first commercial railroad in 1809, a year after I was born.

"As I grew up, I modeled myself after my father. I even chose his profession as my own. I was home-schooled and really only liked mathematics. I acquired my math skills while working on my father's surveys. My father got me my first job. I had thought about going to the military academy at West Point to be trained as a civil engineer, but my Quaker upbringings just wouldn't let me.

"Of course, being home-schooled made me doubt my ability to pass anything at the Academy other than mathematics. One entrance exam was also required to be taken wholly in French. I don't know a single word of it. Besides, my father taught me everything I needed.

"My first job was in 1827 as a rodman on a surveying crew locating the Philadelphia and Columbia Railroad. I was nineteen and living in Valley Forge. I loved it outdoors in the heat and the cold with the animals, the forests, and the adventure. I was young in a profession with unlimited potential and great chances for advancement, even without any formal schooling.

"We surveyed the route for the eighteen-mile canal from Middletown to Columbia, and then began locating the railroad portion of the line from Columbia to Philadelphia. Halfway through, everyone caught malaria, and we had to quit working for three weeks. I have to tell you, I've had two recurrences of the ague since then, but they don't stay with me long. Whenever I'm outside in the elements, I have a chance of a relapse, but I assure you, I can take it. I come back quickly and stronger. It shouldn't bother me down here in the South. You folks never have any cold weather like we do up north.

"I was promoted to principal assistant engineer in 1829 and was in charge of constructing the first twenty miles of road out of Philadelphia. I then became the chief engineer of a locating party on the Camden and Amboy Railroad. I located and surveyed the thirty-six mile eastern division. Afterwards, I worked on numerous special projects for several different roads.

"In 1831 and 1832, I toured England and Scotland to see what innovations they had come up with during the last ten years. I have gained much experience as to railroad practices. What I've learned about steam engines while there could never be learned from a school book.

"And now I'm here in Athens. I apologize for this lengthy discussion of my past, but I felt you should know the complete details of my record and experience, in case you're ever approached by anyone thinking I'm not qualified for this job. I will strive to earn your confidence as soon as my equipment arrives and I can get into the field."

After considering Thomson's background, James Camak immediately called for an initial company stock issue from its subscribers to raise the cash necessary just to get started.

At last the waiting game was over. Thomson's beloved transit was delivered just as promised. The long three-week wait had been both educational and entertaining for a man of his northern upbringing. Thomson knocked out what he had been doing and returned to Augusta. Finally able to work, he and his crew took to the field with five new assistant engineers to make a more precise location of the line. The weather was as bad as it ever had been.

J. EDGAR THOMSON, THE GEORGIA RAIL ROAD YEARS, 1833–1845

Thomson had actually gotten a lot of work done; his downtown office had plenty of room and contained all of the company's surveying equipment that would be needed when the time came. Thomson had also travelled along one of his potential locations of the main line and the Athens branch, and he worked on plans and estimates for the first thirty miles of track leaving Augusta.

Local blacksmiths, many of whom were black men, slaves and free alike, had been selected for the sake of expediency to make the rods, the hammers, and the long crowbars that the gandy dancers would need to lay the track. The gandy dancers, mainly Irishmen imported by Thomson right off the boat, were laborers who got their nickname from the gander-like motions of their arms while they were tamping the ties.

The wagons, rails, spikes, crossties, and ballast would all be ordered soon from local merchants to be used when the final layout had been made and all the transit lines and elevations were settled. Anything of any value could be ordered and readily delivered to any customer by the multitude of merchants in Augusta.

There are so many terrible true stories of enslaved African Americans held in bondage throughout the world. Certainly they can readily be seen in documentaries and movies today. There are a wealth of equally true stories of the personal connection between blacks and whites in America at this early time in our history. Only a fool would be unmindful of the misery caused by the slave trade which brought those unfortunates to our shores. The suffering so many of them endured, the shame and humiliation they shared, and their indignity at not being considered a person, is the greatest shame of our country. But there were many, many uplifting and humane efforts to alleviate some of the terrible pain in which they lived.

The black population of Augusta included more than just the displaced Africans; it also included a lot of free persons of color. Years earlier, during the natives' rebellion in Haiti and Santo Domingo, many black refugees found freedom in Augusta, bringing with them their mixed-blood wives and children. They also brought with them large amounts of compensation from the French government for the lands they had lost. These wealthy blacks who spoke French turned upside down the plantation idea that blacks were only useful to cut wood, haul water, and till fields. These people were carpenters, barbers, wagoners, blacksmiths, boatmen, and millwrights. Their women were seamstresses, house servants, and weavers.

Springfield, on the western edge of Augusta, had been a separate community, but Augusta's growth eventually absorbed it. It was predominantly a black community, but it boasted a tannery, a tobacco warehouse, and a beautiful church. When the white congregation of the Asbury Meeting House desired a new building, they sold the old one to the faithful members of the Springfield Baptist Church. It is now the church's current education building and is the oldest church building in Georgia still in use.

The old Ebenezer Church in Brothersville, between Augusta and Louisville, was originally a branch of the Springfield Baptist Church. Brothersville, today in Richmond County, was named in honor of three brothers: James, Augustus, and Elisha Anderson who built the first homes there. It is called Hephzibah now and was known in the 1800s as Lost Arcadia. During his early ministry, Reverend Charles T. Walker ministered at Ebenezer's altars quite successfully.

In 1848, Colonel A. C. Walker gave to the black citizens a large lot for their religious use. On that lot and through the efforts of the Colonel's most trusted and valued slave, Uncle Frank, a church was built. It was named Franklin Covenant Church in his honor, to perpetuate the name and virtues of that fine man. The Reverend Joseph Walker, its first pastor, was owned by William Evans. After its organization, the church's members raised the necessary funds to buy Joseph Walker's freedom. He then devoted his entire life to ministerial work. Uncle Joe's nephew was asked one time how the church members, all of whom were in bondage, could raise such a large amount of money. Uncle Joe's nephew said, "Well, we raised as much as we could, and our white friends came to our aid with the balance needed."

When Uncle Frank, for whom Franklin Covenant was named, died, his master wrote a sketch of his funeral for the *Home Journal* of New York. "I have lost the best and truest friend I had in this world; one whom I have been accustomed to honor and respect since my earliest childhood. He was the playmate of my father's youth and the mentor of mine, a faithful servant, an honest man, and a sincere Christian.

"I stood by his bedside, and with his hands clasped in mine I heard the last words that he uttered. They were 'Master, meet me in Heaven.' I never spoke a harsh word to him in my entire life, for he never deserved one."

On the other hand, some white Augustans pushed for laws that attempted to force blacks to act like the dependents of whites. The ordinances tried to keep blacks in their place. Only old black folks were allowed to sell goods like beer or cakes.

Any black person, free or slave, could be switched for using insolent language to a white person. Switched, not whipped. The physical pain would be less, but the indignity would never be forgotten in either case. Dancing and drinking in the street by blacks could result in a moderate whipping.

Blacks couldn't have a light in the house past ten. City officials were worried that the blacks could be planning a rebellion. Blacks couldn't sell liquor, smoke a pipe or cigar in public, travel without a pass, learn to read or write, own property, or work in a printing shop. David Drake, the famous slave potter of Edgefield, did learn to read and write and did work in a print shop. His education was known and encouraged by both Abner Landrum and later Lewis Miles, two of his masters during his life.

In 1829, a free Negro from North Carolina, David Walker, published a pamphlet for blacks. His *Walkers' Appeal* called upon blacks to put an end to slavery through insurrection and violence. He scattered copies throughout the South. Southerners called for his arrest and some states called for heavy penalties for circulating the pamphlet. Georgia then passed its law that it was illegal to teach blacks to read and write.

The city would pass those petty laws, but they couldn't, or wouldn't, enforce them. Slave owners wanted everybody, including the city officials and police, to keep their noses out of their business when it came to their slaves. The slave owners readily circumvented those laws by granting, in writing, permission for their slaves to travel, stay up late, attend social events, and live away from the plantation. Augusta didn't have a police force, and no one, including the county sheriffs, knew who had permission and who did not.

Laws were passed that blacks couldn't go into taverns or liquor stores, but the owners of those establishments wanted their business. One said that slaves who were boatmen, or hired themselves out for wages, got money honestly by extra work and should be able to spend it any way they wanted.

One white man complained that slaves were going into retail businesses with white men as partners and that slaves owned several shops in the area. Both were against the law. One ordinance also said that free persons of color could not hire slaves. Whites said that something evil was up when blacks hired blacks. The white people were afraid that the free blacks would encourage the slaves to start an insurrection like Nat Turner's. But the real reason whites didn't like that ordinance was that it repudiated what they had been saying forever - that blacks didn't have enough sense or skill to assume the role of businessmen.

When free blacks were forbidden to hire slaves, they had enough sense to easily take the teeth out of that law. Many of the free blacks started purchasing their own slaves! That really took white officials by surprise, but they never did anything to prevent free blacks from owning slaves.

Against the prevailing white policies, blacks kept on learning. They were helped enormously by white folks, not by missionaries nor by Northerners, but by plain ole simple white Georgians. At the time Edgar Thomson came to town, whites were complaining to the *Augusta Chronicle* about blacks gathering in the city streets on Sundays. Fifth Street between Broad Street and the bridge was their favorite spot.

Whites complained about the black folks meeting at night and on

Sundays at Bridge Row, as they called it. Then they began complaining that the blacks were wearing showy and expensive clothes. They were worried that the blacks were not acting subservient to the whites. Where would that lead?

Blacks were holding formal parties in hotels and public rooms hired for the occasion and in the houses of their understanding masters. Many black women walked the streets of Augusta in calico gowns, plaid shawls, and cloth turbans on their heads. Hearing them calling to each other and laughing loudly, one visitor said that they must think they were the happiest class of people on Earth.

Augusta was a diversified city made up of blacks, whites, Irish, and Jews. Slaves normally lived near their masters, either in their assigned quarters on the plantation or in their little houses behind their masters' homes. Free blacks lived anywhere they wanted, as did the whites.

The Irish had their own neighborhoods between Jackson and Campbell Streets. The local population called the area "Dublin." Just to the west of it was a neighborhood called "Canaan" because of the great number of Jewish folks who lived there. Augusta's Jewish community met for worship in a house on Greene Street at Jackson Street. There was no German neighborhood, as such, but they were growing in number and living between Summerville and Harrisburg.

Augusta had a toll road connecting Augusta to Summerville near the Arsenal. Summerville was not an area populated by any specific groups, but its residents were affluent. It was Augusta's premier residential location.

The tolls from the toll road paid for the cost of the planks and boards, with a little profit added, which made the dirt road both smooth and dry. South of the plank road was Woodlawn, and next to Woodlawn was Harrisonville, the first stop on the railroads' route to Terminus.

Edgar Thomson saw the ease of living among the different races and ethnic groups in Augusta. He surmised that Augusta's way of life was tranquil and cooperative, and slavery was not something about which he should get too upset. His point of view was further confirmed when

Thomson met Richard and Emily Tubman at a charity fundraiser downtown and was asked to become a member of the Augusta Colonizers, a member of the American Colonization Society.

Richard Tubman had stipulated in his will that all his family slaves be given the choice of going to Liberia or staying in Georgia. Sixty-nine slaves chose to undertake the uncertain journey back to Africa. The other two-thirds chose to stay in Augusta and to work for Mrs. Tubman.

Emily Tubman wrote the Society that her people had been liberated based on their fidelity and good conduct. Emily said her slaves — she would have certainly used the word servants — had been brought up as farmers and were skilled in business. They were honest, industrious, and not a one of them was intemperate. She said that every one of them would be an asset to their new country. The liberated slaves all took Tubman as their name, and their settlement in West Africa was called Tubman Hill.

The American Colonization Society's stated mission was to colonize the newly formed nation of Liberia in Africa with freed slaves from the United States. It was so popular in Augusta that it had two chapters, one for women and one for men. Many humane Augustans with their hearts in the right place contributed many thousands of dollars to its cause.

The movement came about when Thomas Jefferson pondered the legacy of slavery. He came to feel that the answer would be to send the blacks back to Africa. Many slave-owners feared the free Negro and, therefore, agreed with him.

The society was headed up by Supreme Court Justice Bushrod Washington, George's nephew. The society recruited members, raised funds, paid agents, and even printed its own newspaper. The only problem with the movement was that it was perceived as racist. People said the underlying assumption of the society was that the Negro was an inferior being, and that the United States, North and South, would be better off without him.

Henry Clay had hoped to repatriate fifty-two thousand Negroes each year. That was, unfortunately, the yearly natural increase in the number of blacks in the nation. It would have been a stalemate, a non-accomplishment, even if that optimistic number was fulfilled. The Colonization Society never sent to Africa more than an insignificant fraction of that number because it did not have the resources to do more.

Many blacks, free men and newly freed slaves, did not want to return to the land of their ancestors. Some slaves even refused their freedom on such terms. It was just as well. Instead of creating a safe haven for any returning slaves, as was the original idea, the new settlers in Liberia, the Tubmans, had a different agenda. They lorded it over the native Africans already living there, and denied them any voice in the government. They acted like the slave masters they had just escaped. They forced the locals to labor as field hands on the farms and on the rubber plantations. The oldest neighborhoods of the elite ruling class, with their beautiful houses reminiscent of New Orleans, are deserted today, their mansions decayed and rotten. William Shadrach Tubman, elected Liberia's President in 1944, ruled with a cruel, autocratic hand for twenty-seven years.

Between 1820 and 1830, only fourteen hundred Negroes were shipped to Liberia, and only two hundred of those were freed slaves. Two million slaves were still left behind.

Thomson responded to Emily Tubman's invitation to join the Society by saying, "I know Judge King is a big supporter of your group, as is Bill Hobby of the *Chronicle*. I encourage these men to support your group, and I have given three thousand dollars to you through them. Those gentlemen are members, but I don't think I need to be an actual member to help out. I am out of town too often to attend regular meetings and functions. I am just too busy. Sorry, but keep up your good work."

Emily Tubman doubled the size of her husband's estate after his death by investing in Georgia Railroad and other industrial stocks. In 1842, she started the first high school for girls in Augusta.

Araminta Ross, born into slavery in 1822 in Maryland, married a free black man in 1844. This man, of whom absolutely nothing else is known, was John Tubman. Immediately after the wedding, Araminta Tubman changed her first name to Harriet, her mother's, to honor her. The newlywed then became known as Harriet Tubman who gained great fame in her later years with the Underground Railroad. Unless I see otherwise, I will always believe that John Tubman was a member of the liberated Tubman clan from Augusta.

3 Lombardy, Raw Whiskey and Weekend Fights

Upon hearing the term "chief engineer," people always thought he was the train's operator, up in the front of the train controlling its speed and blowing the whistle. That man is definitely an engineer, but only a locomotive engineer, someone to be remembered romantically for heroic deeds in the event of the collision of two trains high-balling at fifty miles an hour each.

The chief engineer is the man who is in charge of every aspect of the functioning of the physical railroad. He answers to the board of directors and the president of the company. From the very beginning, the Chief Engineer of the Georgia Rail Road was J. Edgar Thomson, in charge of every small detail concerning the track.

December of 1834 was miserable outside: rainy, cold, and snowy. Adverse events hindered the progress of the survey later on, but Edgar was not going to let a little bad weather keep him from completing the task at hand. Besides, hadn't he said that the South never had any cold weather? On January 5th of 1835, Thomson presented his completed preliminary survey report to James Camak in Athens. Thomson's report, which was released to the public three days later, estimated the construction costs for the first 112 miles of track.

Thomson showed his concern for profit and for the good stewardship of company funds by making a change to the initial route proposed by the Board. By selecting a better route out of Augusta and its surrounding area, Thomson eliminated the need for an inclined plane which was recommended earlier. The city councilmen of Augusta had then transferred to the company Thomson's desired site for its terminal.

Freeman Walker, a well-known and highly respected local activist, and Thomson had become good friends in the short time Thomson had been in Augusta. Born in Virginia, Walker left to study law with his brother in Augusta. After taking a course at the Academy of Richmond County, Walker became a very successful lawyer in town. He began his public career as the intendant of the city. Its name was changed to mayor during his second term. He served three terms and then became a state senator.

Returning to local politics, Walker was elected mayor for the fourth time. He also served very faithfully as a trustee of St. Paul's Protestant Episcopal Church and of the Richmond Academy School Board. Henry Clay, during his visit to Augusta in 1844, declared Walker's home on the corner of Greene and Washington Streets to be the prettiest home in town. Walker became an integral part of Augusta and its history forever when he sold his country house, a magnificent family plantation in Summerville, in 1826 to President John Quincy Adams, as fiduciary for the United States. The government was the recipient of the site for the newly relocated military Arsenal at Augusta. Bellevue, the plantation's beautiful residence, is still as lovely today as it was when the Walkers owned it.

According to Document No. 96 of the 19th Congress, entitled *Message from the President of the United States… in Relation to the Site of the Arsenal of the United States at Augusta, in the State of Georgia*, dated February 17, 1826, the unhealthiness of the Augusta Arsenal required immediate attention. "A change of position to a healthy situation is demanded by a just regards to the health of the troops…. The original site was selected and purchased in 1816. The buildings were commenced in May, 1818. The workmen continued healthy throughout that year. In 1819, the place proved to be very unhealthy. The sickness commenced early in July, and continued until late in

November, and nineteen of the workmen became ill.... The position chosen for the Arsenal is at present unhealthy beyond a doubt. A tract of flat ground in the vicinity, covered with stagnant water the greater part of the year, is imagined to be the cause of the insalubrity of the spot."

The grounds around the Arsenal were drained in an effort to cure the problem, but it was not successful. Almost every year, "the troops have been removed from the Arsenal to the 'Sand Hills,' about one and a half miles, for about four months in each year."

Major M. M. Payne reported to Congress on October 1, 1825, "I regret to state that circumstances have compelled me to remove the garrison from the Arsenal. About the 17th Sept. a fever of a most alarming character made its appearance at this post. Ass't Surgeon, Dr. T. P. Hall was attacked on the 17th, and died on the morning of the 21st of yellow fever.... I therefore directed the Quartermaster to rent a house on the Sand Hills, for the reception of the sick, retaining at the post only three well men of the command... I feel it is my duty to report, that I have not, at this time, a single man capable of performing a day's duty."

Eventually, during the 1820 Yellow Fever epidemic in Augusta, almost every enlisted man and officer of the garrison at the old Augusta Arsenal at Harrisburg died. Only the commandant survived. Mathew Payne, the garrison commander, was visiting the Walker family at Bellevue when the fever hit. Payne contracted the yellow plague but was saved the fate his men endured because the Walkers nursed him back to health. Recovered, Payne contributed his good fortune to being on the Hill when the epidemic began. Convinced of the healthy benefits of living on the Hill, Payne started talking to Walker about the possibility of selling the Walker home to the government for the relocation of the arsenal. It would be for the good of his country, Payne said, but what would it mean to the Walkers? Reluctantly, Freeman Walker decided to sell all seventy-two acres of land, except one, and his two buildings to the government for six thousand dollars. The one acre remains in the family for all time as their family burial plot.

Maybe the Federal government and its military were pleased with the purchase, and maybe the Walkers were pleased with the sale, but the people of Summerville were beside themselves with hatred about the whole thing. What Summerville resident wanted a noisy, busy bunch of soldiers marching and shouting all over their peaceful, quiet pasture land and beautiful woods? Eventually those folks got their wish. After the arsenal had been closed for many years, Augusta University made the land and its buildings their beautiful, quiet home.

Over lunch at one of their favorite eating establishments downtown, known locally as the Town Tavern, Walker asked Thomson how his railroad was shaping up. Thomson smiled, "It has begun well. I've made a few changes for the good of the company. In my latest report to the Board, I have given them my predictions of future earnings once the road is finished. This is a little like tooting my own horn, but it makes for great job security for me. It also inspires them to agree with me. What director can complain about our operations and our tremendous spending when the results look so profitable? I will keep doing this until we are complete."

After considering Thomson's optimistic report, James Camak called for another stock issue to fund Thomson's field work. Thomson returned to Augusta and into the field with five new assistant engineers to make a more precise location of the line. The weather was as bad as it ever had been.

Adiel Sherwood's *Gazetteer of Georgia* reported on the night of January 8th, eight inches of snow fell. No one could recall such a depth. On February 3rd, four more inches of snow fell; the temperature plunged to minus ten degrees, and Thomson was forced to seek shelter. The cold weather in New England began on about the 25th of January, but it did not reach Georgia until the 7th of February. On February 8th, the mercury showed three degrees below zero in Eatonton and eight below in Milledgeville. Nothing like this had ever been known in Georgia. In Florida, it was not as severe until the 4th of March, when most of the orange trees were killed.

The Southern Banner reported it was so cold that two black people froze to death in Athens. It snowed the entire week of March 5th, and three days of the following week as well. By mid-March, six to eight inches of snow still covered the ground, but Thomson and his surveying crew still slogged on.

The weather was not Thomson's only problem. The land the men were working through was woods and farmland. There were a few small hamlets here and there, but basically, between Augusta and Washington and Greensboro, there were few signs of anything other than open land and a few taverns. Only the town of Wrightsboro had anything professing it to be something other than a cow pen. In other areas, taverns were operated to feed and shelter the wagoners travelling between Augusta and all points west. The taverns were usually quite profitable, and the locals depended upon that income.

Thomson told William Dearing, "My assistant engineers, our men and I are being boarded at the few local houses and taverns along the route. It gets quite crowded at times, but it can't be prevented. Even in this terrible cold and snow, the survey line is being laid out daily. We have progressed from Augusta through Harrisonville to Bell Air, Berzelia, and Lombardy. There was very little in these places when we slogged through except trees and bushes and an occasional house or two. It's hard living when you have to break the ice in the water pitcher in your room on these mornings, but it's better than sleeping in the ice."

In 1773, more than sixty years earlier, the Augusta—Wrightsboro Road was declared a public thoroughfare by the state. John Stubbs and Isaac Lowe from Wrightsboro were appointed overseers to keep the road in the Wrightsboro area in good repair. Throughout the state, it was required of all abled-bodied men from fifteen to thirty to contribute twelve days of labor a year in road maintenance.

Anticipating the surveying party's arrival, some of the local inhabitants of these hamlets had met to discuss the new railroad coming through. The discussions became heated as they began to realize that what was once thought to be a great upcoming event for their future could actually do them harm. The landowners, farmers, and tavern owners along the route being surveyed began to fear the construction of a railroad. They knew it threatened their profitable business of providing the food, shelter, and supplies for the long-haul wagoners on their road.

No railroad was needed anywhere in Georgia, the local people selfishly felt, because their villages got their fair share of carriage and wagon traffic from the business dealings and commerce between Augusta and Athens. When the surveyors reached these places, they were face to face with a mutinous gang of Georgia tavern keepers, landowners, and minor merchants.

The inhabitants had become so hostile and insulting at the thought of losing business to the future rail lines that Thomson had to resort to arming his men for their protection. He thought, "*Other railroad engineers have to arm themselves against hostile Indians, but I've got to protect my men from the damned scoundrels around here.*" He also had to purchase tents and living equipment so his surveying party could live in the field.

The greatest source of the animosity of these displaced folks occurred in the hamlet of Lombardy, later renamed for the company's future President, William Dearing. In the time it had taken the surveying crew to sight the first twenty-five miles of future track, these backwoods Georgia farmers had figured it out. It hadn't taken them too long. They were uneducated but they weren't dumb; this new railroad was going to be bad news economically for a lot of them in the short term.

Lombardy wasn't the only source of trouble. The town of Lexington objected to the railroad on account of the noise and the fact that it frightened the livestock. They passed a law stating the railroad could not pass within four miles of the city limits. The Augusta Board of Trade stipulated, before they gave the railroad its blessings, that the road had to terminate in Augusta and that it could not go on to Savannah. They also stipulated that the railroad could in no way compete with the boat trade on the Savannah River.

Thomson collared a young assistant engineer, Billy Wells, and made him accompany him to Lombardy to see if they could talk some sense into what he was sure were the usually kind and understanding farmers there. Thomson didn't know just how bad Lombardy's reputation was. Gathering near the four wooden buildings which served as the town, Thomson and Wells heard a tremendous shouting and hooting from the crossroads in the hamlet's center. It came from a crowd in the dusty dirt street in front of old man Neal's storehouse, the scene of many a drunken brawl.

Augustus Baldwin Longstreet, the South's premier man of letters, compiled many wonderful stories of the actual life and times in and around Augusta in the 1830s. He had first written them and had them published in newsprint from October of 1833 to March of 1835. Longstreet's stories appeared in book form in 1835 when they were published as *Georgia Scenes, Characters, Incidents, & in the First Half Century of the Republic*. The author was stated as a "Native Georgian" which didn't fool any of the Georgia crowd who had read them earlier in their paper. It took the rest of the country a little later to figure it out.

The publisher of the original volume was Longstreet's own company, the State Rights' Sentinel. The book was considered a masterpiece and Edgar Allen Poe, for one, could not get over how great it was. It was the birth of realistic humorous literature in America. Mark Twain followed its style to the letter.

"My God, Billy, we have stumbled upon the actual scene of Mr. Longstreet's story 'The Fight.' I have just read it in the *Sentinel*," Thomson said.

In the center of a circular ring of ropes in the middle of the crossroads, two huge men were brawling. The two men had heard of each other, but had always kept their distance, just to prevent this. At this time, the Saturday entertainment for the local farmers was called rough-and-tumble fighting, or eye-gouging. In an earlier time, eye-gouging accompanied the brawling, but to their credit the people of Lombardy had forbidden that unholy practice in recent years. Fighters were separated as soon as someone tried to pull that.

This was an accepted, yet horrendous, type of fighting in the backwoods of our nation. It began in the 1700s and continued across America until, by the time it reached Missouri, it was on the wane. The sport, if it could be called that, was usually used to settle local scores and insults. Here, it was undertaken for the pure joy of it during a Saturday afternoon. It would later remind Thomson of going to a community horse race. No one was killed, but many men were disfigured or maimed for life. With the advent of pistols and Bowie knives for dueling, and under the guidance of the church and pressure from the local ladies, rough-and-tumble finally faded out in the hamlets and villages, including the good village of Lombardy.

Thomson told Billy, "Mr. Longstreet said the fight in his story started when the wives of the two toughest men in town were railroaded into it by a trouble-maker. The wives had simultaneously dropped into the only store in town, and both demanded to be waited on first. The two men were in town with their separate militia battalions from around the county participating in a regimental parade. Longstreet said that a hundred gamecocks will live in perfect harmony together if you do not put a hen in with them. But that's what happened.

"One woman told the owner to wait on her first. The other said she was in a hurry and she wanted to be waited on first. One lady asked who the other was. The reply was, 'Your betters, madam.'

"One husband walked in and said, 'Let's go, it's getting late.' His wife said she would have been ready a half-hour ago if it hadn't been for that impudent hussy. 'Who do you call an impudent hussy, you nasty, good-for-nothing, snaggle-toothed gob of fat, you?'

"The husband said, 'Look here, woman, have you got a husband here? If you have, I'll lick him till he learns to teach you better manners, you sassy heifer, you.' At that, the local trouble-maker flew out of the store, went to the other husband, and said he needed to hurry to save his wife.

"The husband sprang to the store, followed by a hundred friends, for a bully never wants for friends. As he entered the store, the man asked the first husband what he had said to his wife. The first husband replied that it was enough for a fight. The new arrival asked if the first husband was ready for a fair fight. 'Yes, I am; I've heard much of your manhood, but I believe I am a better man than you,' was the reply.

"The circular rope ring was made, and the men entered, shirtless. Each battalion gathered near its champion. One of the seconds stepped up and said, 'Gentlemen, I understand it is to be a fair fight; catch as catch can; rough and tumble.' Are you ready? We are ready. 'Then blaze away, my gamecocks!'"

Billy was mesmerized by the story Thomson was remembering from the paper. Thomson detailed the fight as best he could. It was hard to believe that such a civilized man could retell it with such gusto.

"Bob rushed at Bill and flipped Bill on his head. Shouts and screams burst from the lower battalion as Bill smashed his head upon the ground. Bill was the much larger, better endowed man of the two, but Bob was quick and dexterous, with nothing to be ashamed of in his physique. Bob's battalion roared to Bill's friends, 'Save him,' 'Feed him,' 'Give him the Durham physic till his stomach turns!' Dr. Durham made his home-made medicines in Frogpond, the next town over.

"The men could not get away from each other to stand up, so they lay there head to head for a while, like there was nothing to do. Then by mutual consent they stood. One look at Bob's face and someone shouted, 'Look yonder, didn't I tell you so. Bob hit his face on the ground so hard, it jarred his nose off.'" Bob had lost his entire left ear and a large piece from his left cheek. Bill was a hideous spectacle. A third of the lower extremity of his nose was bit off. They were up only for a second and then down they went again.

"Bill seemed to have an advantage because he had his arm tightly around Bob's neck. He let go of it surprisingly, but it became clear when they rose again. Bill had the middle finger of Bob's left hand in his mouth, and therefore he wasn't able to pound Bob's body with both hands. Bill's blows got weaker after the first three or four, and it became clear that Bill needed the room that Bob's finger occupied in his mouth for breathing. He would have to let it go shortly, but Bob was nice enough to jerk his hand away and present Bill with the present of his finger.

"Time and again the men rose and fell. They were exhausted and fell once more. After a short pause, Bob gathered his hand full of dirt and sand, and was in the act of grinding it into Bill's eyes, when Bill cried, 'Enough.'"

"Longstreet said language cannot describe the scene that followed. Many small fights broke out between the battalions as the champions were carried away and were washed off. Both men were bed ridden for two weeks, but they met again soon after that and shook hands. They eventually became good friends. It had just been another day in town."

Thomson turned to his side and spied a young man deeply engrossed in the fight. He did not seem to be very intoxicated, so Thomson asked him how he knew when the whole shebang was over. Robert Printup, the gentleman under interrogation, said, "Whenever someone has had enough, they yell 'Enough' or 'Boys, take him off of me.' Then they are separated. Wait a minute and you'll see what happens.

"Bill, being the loser, will have to buy a gallon of cheap whiskey for everybody to quench their thirst, as they say. Y'all are welcome to some of it. It ain't store bought, but that's what makes it so good. By the time that gallon's finished, there'll be another fight and then another gallon, and then another fight and another gallon, all day long.

"If somebody gets too drunk to fight, we just drag him under old man Neal's store until he's able to get up and join the fray again. I don't want you guys to get the wrong idea. This is not an everyday thing. These are hardworking, good farmers who work hard five days a week. They come to town every Saturday to finish up the week's work with this fun."

Thomson and Billy Wells edged to where the men were washing up. It was crowded, packed with humanity that smelled like dirt and manure and liquor. Printup was right; it was Saturday and many of the men had come to town to get something to drink and chew the fat. It was the strong drink and the hot noonday sun that caused most of them to get drunk. It was nothing unusual.

The town ladies were few and far between. They were sick and tired of having a son or a husband coming home drunk and filthy and maimed. Thomson approached one lady and asked where did this crazy tradition arise? The lady looked at Thomson and replied, "They've always done it; some of it's from the Bible."

"What are you talking about, woman? What has the Bible to do with any of this?"

"Well, gouging out eyes is mentioned many times in the Bible. What about Samson? He called on the Lord to strengthen him just one more time so he could avenge the Philistines for gouging out both his eyes. What about in Samuel when Nahash the Ammonite went up and besieged Jabesh. The besieged men asked what it would take to make a treaty with Nahash and then they would serve him like slaves. Nahash said to them that only on one condition would he make a treaty, and that condition would be that he would gouge out the right eye of everyone in the city, and thereby put disgrace upon all Israel. Of course, Saul came to their rescue after a few days and killed every Ammonite warrior. That's the way it was in the old days in the Bible. Thank God, our men stopped eye-gouging a few years ago. It was horrendous."

"Lady, what's your name? You know an awful lot about the Bible. Are you a preacher?"

"Heavens, no. We don't even have a church here and our men are too hung over, or just plain sorry, to drive us to Sweetwater Baptist over near Frogpond on worship day. I wish I had a stack of Bibles right here. I'd swear on every one that within a year I'm getting us a building for worship and a circuit rider, and pleased to meet you. My name is Jennie Clark.

"But I'll tell you what the problem is: whiskey. Whiskey is that hateful evil that steals men of their reason and murders their wives and their children. Then it takes those men's own lives away. It's the grog that crowds our asylums and penitentiaries and sends millions of souls to hell each year. I do wish I had just one man around here, though, who felt the same. We women are getting tired of not having one thing for us to do except washing, cooking, sewing, having babies, picking vegetables, and waiting on our men folk like children. I wish we had some control over something in our lives."

Thomson thought a moment and said to her, "Have you read the old classic book about the ancient women who had your same problem? They couldn't stop their men from fighting either. And how they cured it?"

"No, we don't have enough time in the day, except it appears on Saturdays, to do anything but work. The only book any of us have to read is the Good Book. What'd those women do?"

"Well, their men wouldn't quit fighting; it was just in their blood. They weren't drunk or anything, they just always had to fight their neighbors. So the women got together. They ran all the prostitutes in town out and told the men that they wouldn't be having any more sex until they changed their lifestyle. That is, unless it was with each other. The women won, and the men finally found other things to do with their spare time besides constantly going out and killing each other. That was three or four thousand years ago in ancient Greece or Rome, I don't remember."

Mrs. Clark told Thomson what a wonderful idea that was and that she was going to try it, and soon. She believed it would work. Thomson told Wells to get ready to go back to Augusta. Billy asked if they weren't going to talk to any of the men about treating the railroad personnel better, which was why they had come in the first place.

Billy said he had asked around and had some names of upstanding God-fearing folks who might help keep the animosity down. It wouldn't even be a stretch to call them Christians, Billy thought. His list included Uncle Jack Harris, Steven Drane, Green Reeves, and Buck Phillips.

Billy said some other men could help, but they didn't attend the fights and stayed at home on Saturdays. It would be too much trouble to hunt them down at their homes. They included Captain Willis Howard, William Printup, George W. Rodgers, and Dr. D. A. Rodgers. Wells told

Thomson that Captain Howard was one of the hamlet's earliest settlers and largest landowner. He was told by almost everyone that Howard was a great soldier and militia man.

Thomson asked Billy, "Where was that Dr. Rodgers today? He could have sewn up some cheeks and noses. Let's go; I'm not coming back to Lombardy again until that church is built."

Louis LeClerc Milfort in his *Memoirs* would have reassured Edgar Thomson that he would find men such as these anywhere in the frontier of America at this time. Milfort says that throughout his twenty years in our country's frontier and Indian lands, he often came across Crackers, or Gougers, as they were called, and who were nearly all one-eyed.

Jennie Clark was right; the cause of that evil was whiskey, whiskey made from home grown potatoes. The Crackers were very fond of it, and since they were mean and quarrelsome by nature, they fought like the devil when drunk on that rotgut. A big crowd was gathered, a circle was formed, and the fight was on.

The men from their infancy never cut the fingernails of their little fingers. They smeared them with tallow and held them in front of the fire to harden them. Some were as hard as the claws of a lion. The men also armed themselves by wearing spurs on their heels. They never took them off, even to go to bed, and their rosette was a very sharp pointed spike.

The older of the two Crackers would yell, "Anything is allowed," and the fight would begin. They used their teeth, their spurs, and their fingernails. When one of the two men was knocked down, the other inhumanely tore him to pieces and took out an eye.

The onlookers watched the fight very calmly until an eye was ruined, and then they quickly jumped in to pull the men apart. The civilized and educated folks must have thought it would have been unchristian and animal-like if both eyes of a fighter were torn out. Besides, why would a man on the frontier in the 1830s need two eyes?

At this time in the early to mid-1850s, America was a hard-drinking country. The consumption of raw whisky was brutal and devastating, especially on the frontier. Dr. Benjamin Rush published a book on the terrible effects of alcohol on the mind and body of a drinker and gave mortality statistics on those afflicted.

The book was an instant best-seller and its readership spread throughout the country. Reformers told of alcohol's link with poverty and crime. They said intemperance was the sin of the land, even equal to slavery. In Boston, there was one grogshop, or bar, for every twenty-one males over the age of sixteen.

The local Congregational and Presbyterian churches finally rose up and formed the Massachusetts Society for the Suppression of Intemperance. It was the prototype for America's Intemperance Movement, which eventually found its way to the sunny South, much to the pleasure of Jennie Clark and her girlfriends.

4 Cap' Wilson, Frogpond, and Wrightsboro

Three or four miles on the west side of the six houses of Boneville, where the engineers did not stop to talk with anyone, the men came to a lovely, large plantation owned by Captain John Wilson. Mr. Wilson's family had possessed this land since receiving it on July 3, 1770, by a grant from the British Colonial Governor, Sir James Wright.

The Wilsons and their ancestors, the Thomas Watsons, had all been very loyal to the Crown before the American Revolution, just as most of the country's population had been. They felt that only the presence of British troops of war could keep their neighboring Indians from killing them and stealing their horses. They had a great fear of these marauding Indians, and for good reason.

During the Revolutionary War, this region of Georgia in which Edgar Thomson was now surveying had seen more partisan murder and destruction than all the rest of Georgia combined. It was properly called the Hornet's Nest to reflect the churning, stinging, biting war wherein brother killed brother, and no one was safe from reprisal. Half the deaths here had occurred at the point of a pistol or a rifle held in the hands or arms of a once-beloved neighbor or kinsman.

During the war, people's allegiance shifted occasionally, depending on the current events of their region. A staunch Loyalist was willing to fight with the British to keep law and order in his countryside if he believed only the British could maintain the law. Keeping law and order was a legitimate reason to support the king, especially if one were the owner and master of a magnificent plantation. Believing that the British would keep the savages at bay was another good reason to side with them. But some men such as Wilson would change loyalty and fight with the Patriots for freedom from Britain. It usually happened if it appeared that the Patriots, unbelievably, had a chance to win, or if some renegade Loyalist militia had hanged their father, or a son, on a tree in their yard in front of their children.

Most Loyalists and their families were banished after the war, and their land and property was given to deserving, liberty-loving, hard-fighting Patriots. The land was parceled out to the Patriots in bounty grants of 287 and a half acres each. Loyalists were forced, or chose, to leave; many went to Canada, many went back to England, and many set up new lives in the Caribbean.

After the war, Georgia lawmakers softened the banishment and confiscation acts for some people. Those people who had helped the British out of sheer self-defense and preservation were pardoned outright and allowed to stay in Georgia. Some of those were fined ten percent of their holdings, but, unfortunately, their lands and property, if previously given to a Patriot, were not returned to them.

Captain John Wilson came home to his beloved Pine Top, as it would later be known, after the war. He and the men in his family had all fought in the 3rd South Carolina Battalion in the Continental Army. They were all honest men and soldiers, full of pride, supporting their new nation. They had not engaged in the cold-blooded killing of rival families or personal enemies in the area as so many of the Patriots and the Loyalists had done. They had not become men who took the law into their own hands like the Regulators who were both judge and jury whenever they chose.

Fifty-three years later, as Thomson's party came sloshing through the snow and mud, these people were just as stern and hard as ever they had been. They believed in their rights and they wanted no outside interference of any kind which might lead to a change in their lives. To many of them, that included a railroad. The weather was beginning to warm up a little; maybe it would warm a few hearts.

Captain John Wilson understood the problems Thomson was having with the local inhabitants along the proposed line, and he was sympathetic, especially since he thought he could possibly make a dollar somehow by being sympathetic.

Wilson agreed to put up Thomson and his assistant engineers in his house for a day or a week, as needed, as they worked along the line. Wilson would provide the engineers with room, board, warm fireplaces, heated water, and companionship, for free. He did, however, think that the Georgia Rail Road Company should be more than happy to pay to have their survey crews rooming in Wilson's cabins and eating Wilson's food during their stay. He hoped the railroad would pay dearly, not that he was greedy.

The cabins were each alike, painted red with white trim, and were used to house the Wilsons' slaves. In one larger and much nicer cabin standing a hundred yards from the others lived the white overseer, Jim Morgan, and his family. They were not inconvenienced by the rentals to the Thomson party.

The slaves, on the other hand, were very much inconvenienced but were very generous in not complaining about having to move into eight of the fifteen cabins to make accommodations for the surveyors. What good would it do to complain? Slave owners generally agreed how accommodating most slaves were, whatever their reason for being that way. After a quick sweeping and splashing of water to the walls and floors, the cabins were ready for any person, black or white. Any person, that is, who may have been working from sunrise until sunset in freezing weather out in the elements without a bath or change of clothes in six weeks.

Cap' Wilson drove Thomson in his finest carriage along the stagecoach route to the next plantation, a fine farming operation owned by

John Langston. Adjoining Langston's spread to the west were three wood framed houses with old log cabins in the back. These one-story, unpainted and dirty houses were placed on the corners of two crossroads; one connecting Wrightsboro to Indian land and the other connecting Augusta to Madison.

This hamlet was called Frogpond, but with the opening of the railroad, it was later incorporated as the village of Thomson in honor of Edgar Thomson. "I've heard people say I was bribed into running our line through here, but that would have had no effect on me. That little hamlet of Frogpond was named Thomson because I was one of the officials of the road, as were Dearing and Camak. We wouldn't have had even a depot in Thomson except our locomotives needed to stop near there to take on wood and water. You can't run a steam locomotive very far without wood and water."

Once the railroad construction was begun and the rails were laid, the water tower in Frogpond would be built. The wood for powering the steam engines would require sheds to cut it and to keep it dry. Men would be needed to operate both facilities. People would be needed to feed and shelter these men and themselves. Blacksmiths, merchants, tavern keepers and stables for horses and wagons would be required. This is how towns grew from nothing to become places of businesses, offices, and residences. In May of 1838, the future appeared when a post office was established in the Langston home.

In 1842, Joseph Stockton, a surveyor employed by the railroad, moved to Thomson from Augusta. By that time, the train was operational beyond Frogpond, and the village boasted a house, a merchant, and a blacksmith shop. But it was a long way from being a town. The water tower and railroad yard were maintained by local hired slaves. The slaves were the property of Langston, but he allowed them to work as they were needed under the direction of a railroad employee. They made sure the tower was full of clean water and the wood was in ample supply. They were allowed to keep their railroad wages since they only worked part-time after their regular chores were done.

Langston did a good business in tar; in the winter he kept his slaves busy with collecting fat wood or resinous pine. They would make piles of it, and when a pile got rather large, they would dig a ditch around it. They would slope the ditch downward to a basin at its bottom. The wood would be lighted and tar would flow out of it. The slaves took the tar out of the basin and placed it into large barrels. Two hundred large barrels of tar could be gathered from one large pile of pine.

Before using the pine for tar, the slaves would draw the turpentine from it. They would make a sloping hole in the body of the tree about a foot above the ground. They put a vessel under the hole to catch the sap running from it. Every morning the slaves would go to collect the liquid and pour it into large barrels. The sap becomes the turpentine.

This tapping was usually done only when the sap was running up the tree. The tree was usually killed by this process, but as it died, it became very resinous and made fat pine which was then used for tar. It was quite an operation and one that was usually done by competent indentured servants bonded for life.

Mr. Stockton caught the eye of Mr. Langston's daughter and married her in 1846. With the scarcity of available ladies to behold, she may have been the only available white female within thirty-five miles. Stockton, an early visionary, acquired a large parcel of land to the south of the railroad tracks and divided the land into building lots. Stockton became Frogpond's first real estate developer when he started to sell the building lots in town. He built several homes and businesses. The most notable commercial building he constructed was the Greenway Hotel in 1850, which later became the Knox Hotel.

Cap' Wilson had such an easy-going way with folks that Edgar Thomson expressed an interest in having Wilson accompany him down the line to talk with the other landowners. Thomson had earlier, in a preliminary survey, tried to take his road through the town of Wrightsboro, but the people of the village were of the same opinion as other landowners who did not want it.

During a nice letup in the weather, Thomson asked Wilson to take him to Wrightsboro in his carriage to give those stiff-necked farmers one more chance at what would obviously be their future fame and fortune. Thomson was impressed that Wrightsboro had a fine church which was shared by any and all faiths of its citizens, an academy for learning built in 1826, thirty houses, and several shops.

Wrightsborough, as originally spelled, was named for England's Royal Governor of Georgia, Sir James Wright. By edict of Royal Governor James Wright in 1763, this group of Quakers was granted 40,000 acres of good timber and farm land surrounding the place where this fledgling town was established. In 1754, Edmund Grey had established a hamlet called Brandon on this same land which was still legally a part of Native American ancestral land. Grey and his followers moved on in 1755, abandoning the hamlet.

The Wrightsboro Quakers had their religious meetings in their homes until they built their first meeting house around 1770. Due to harassment by the Indians and a couple of bad growing seasons, nearly a third of the original settlers of all faiths had left by 1771. Almost twenty years later most Quakers were ostracized by the other townsmen of Wrightsboro because the Quakers had not fought against the British in the Revolution. Of course, they had not fought with the British, either, but that didn't matter to these hot-headed, unforgiving, stiff-necked frontiersmen.

Quakers followed some strict rules of conduct; these were the same that Edgar Thomson had learned as a child. They could be expelled from their Society of Friends for marrying out of the society, for not paying their debts, for playing cards, for bearing arms in a war-like manner, for marrying within five months of their spouse's death, and for hiring a slave.

That was hiring a slave, not owning a slave, which would have been the ultimate sin, but early Quakers had owned slaves. At their yearly meeting in 1774, these original Quakers of Wrightsboro had been ordered to set all their slaves free, or they would be dismissed from the Society.

One of the earliest original merchants in Wrightsboro was the wealthy

Benjamin Rees. The old grist mill built by Joseph Maddox at Maddocks Creek was sold in 1805 to Hugh Rees, Benjamin's son. The beautiful Methodist Church, built in 1810, was the showcase of the village whose population had shrunk to a thousand by this time.

John Louis Porter published the village's only newspaper, *The Village Wreathe*, in 1820, and it ran through the 1850s. Sherwood Roberts operated the Wrightsboro Inn primarily for the benefit of travelers.

When the stagecoach line ran from Augusta to Athens, it passed through Wrightsboro and then on to Washington. The inn was an important stopping place for the passengers on board. Each passenger paid a stage fare of $9 for the entire ninety-three mile trip which only covered 20 to 30 miles each day.

The stagecoaches carried the United States mail, too. One corner of the inn's main room had a desk with a backdrop of pigeonholes and a chair. This was used as the official Wrightsboro post office. Before the stagecoach line, the mail was carried on horseback.

The pride of the town was its acclaimed academy for boys; its instructors had included Moses Waddell, Billington Sanders, and Columbus Richards, to name a few. Moses Waddell founded the Wrightsboro academy in 1794, moved to South Carolina to found the famous Willington School in 1804, and became the University of Georgia's fifth President in 1819. Billington Sanders was the Dean of the Wrightsboro academy and left in 1833 to become the first President of Mercer University in Penfield.

Columbus C. Richards was the head of the academy, newly named the Male Academy, in the 1840s. Columbus was known as a great instructor, but he had a quick temper. He was a strict disciplinarian and fully believed in whipping disobedient pupils. Parents from all over Georgia sent their problem boys to Mr. Richards who would not tolerate any foolishness from those juvenile delinquents. Richard's specialty was making the soon-to-be disciplined boy go down to the creek bank and cut his own switch. Mr. Richards was a well-respected teacher during his career in

Wrightsboro, in Thomson in present day McDuffie County, and in Summerville in present day Emanuel County.

In 1793, Eli Whitney invented the cotton gin, but it was not perfected and was unusable until he uncovered its secret during a visit to Augusta. The cotton gin gave planters the ability to process cotton cheaply and efficiently. That encouraged them to increase their acreage planted in cotton, which required them to increase the number of slaves to cultivate it. The Quakers of Wrightsboro began their exodus when they found they could not compete with slave labor.

So there was only a small population of the original group of Quakers still residing in Wrightsboro when Thomson came through. The folks who had remained had given up their faith and the necessity of living in a Quaker community. They had too many other ties to Georgia to leave in 1806 during the general Quaker exodus to Ohio, Indiana, and points west.

Thomson's parents had both been raised as Quakers, but for some reason they had gotten married in an Episcopal Church. Thomson had been taught to live with Quaker values, so it must have been traumatic for him to have his men issued weapons that could kill another human. Quakers did not believe in taking another's life because they believed there was a little bit of God in everybody. Therefore, if you killed any person, you would be killing a little bit of God.

In his later life, Thomson would always be considered a Quaker because he signed all his personal and business documents as "I affirm" and never as "I swear." Quakers believed that if someone had to swear to prove that they were telling the truth at a particular time, even in a courtroom, it would mean that without that vow they may not be telling the truth at other times.

After Thomson's overview of Wrightsboro, Captain Wilson introduced Thomson all around. "I am amazed, Cap', it seems you know everybody."

"I should, Mr. Thomson. I work with these good people almost daily. I sell them horses, foodstuff, saddles, supplies, plants, and animals on trade or for what little cash there is floating around here. I'll be seventy-eight years old soon and I have seen it all in this country. When I speak, people around here listen."

For whatever reason, Edgar Thomson could not entice the leaders of Wrightsboro into agreeing to let the railroad go through town. "Mr. Thomson, we have talked with other landowners and they have told us that other owners had been swindled and underpaid when they had dealt with the railroads. We just don't want to deal with all the confusion and distrust."

The townsmen added, "We love our fields, our woods, our homes, and our quiet. We have a good church, a good trading post, a good stagecoach road, good water, and good friends. What more could a man want or need?" This would be their eventual downfall. The town would wither up and die.

Years later, Thomson would remember the quiet, almost secret, conversations Wilson had with the townsmen when Thomson was engaged likewise with another group. He would ask himself if ole Cap' Wilson sabotaged his plan of going through Wrightsboro so that the railroad would then have to go through Cap's land. No one ever said Captain Wilson was not a crafty businessman.

Cap' Wilson had a genuine affection for Thomson and was moved one evening to invite him to join the local landowners and a few select farmers and business men to the next morning's fox-hunt. Although he had been planning to return to Augusta and catch up on some bill-paying and contract reviews, Thomson changed his mind and accepted.

5 The Fox-Hunt at Foxboro

The morning came, as evidenced by the hustle and bustle of the household's clattering and banging during the preparation of breakfast for the hunters. "Good morning, Thomson," Cap' Wilson blustered, "We're going to have great sport today! There's nothing in the world greater than a fox-hunt. You'll see.

"Squire Hicks is already here. I'll introduce you to him shortly; he's outside with the horses. Charlie will be here shortly with his dogs. We'll have a pack of twenty or thirty of the best dogs you ever saw. Get some breakfast. Try those eggs and bacon with some grits. I knew there was something noble about you, Mr. Thomson, when you told me last week how much you liked grits."

Outside, Thomson found a lovely morning; the frost covered the ground like a sheet of glass or the morning dew. The stars still glowed in the sky. Since no one had helped him, Thomson was trying to find a horse for himself. One of the servants, as the people of the South always called their slaves, approached Thomson and asked if he had selected a mount.

"Yes, I think I'd like this one if he is unattached."

"Master, you think you gwine fox-hunting on that hoss?"

"Yes, why?"

"He-he," chuckled the servant.

Thomson asked, "What's so funny?"

"Bess da Lord. This old nag neber made for fox-hunting, I do declare. He too lazy, massa. Time one hound give a squall, dey done leff you clean outen sight an' hearing. You mite as well stay inside. He-he, I know."

"Oh, that's okay. I don't plan on keeping up with the dogs; I'll just hang back and cut across back and forth watching and hearing them. Saddle him up and let's get on with it." Thomson would remember later that he wished he had asked for a whip or spur, or both. Thomson had been quite a horseman years earlier as he labored in the elements during his Pennsylvania surveying engagements. In the excitement of all the events unfolding around him on that morning, Thomson had forgotten it all.

The leader of the hunt, Epp, blew his horn and it was answered by several from neighboring hills. Epp was one of Cap' Wilson's four sons. He wore a splendid blood-red waistcoat and rode a beautiful, well-manicured stallion. His word was the law during the hunt. He also occasionally assisted the hunt's houndsman when things got hectic.

As Thomson approached the rendezvous point at Foxboro, many horns and bugles announced that everyone was assembled except Thomson; he had been forgotten in the excitement, but he didn't mind. Half the assembled group were local landowners who let the hunt trample all over their property. The other half were members of the hunt club and their guests. The club had members from eight different states and England. The matriarch of the hunt was a local legend known for her wit, her pleasantness, and her poetry. Thomson was surprised at how much he enjoyed the friendship of the hunters.

Thomson quickly realized that ole Isaac's prediction and his grasp of the aged and infirmed horse he was on was totally correct. The horse moseyed along at a very gentle pace. Thomson requested a little more speed with the click of his heels, and the horse responded, but just barely. Once again Thomson asked for more pace. Once again it was insufficiently supplied. The third time Thomson used his heels upon the horse's flanks; the horse stopped and turned around. It was heading for home when Thomson regained control.

Everyone was there when Thomson finally arrived. There was a slight holdup before the hunt commenced. There was a dog fight, or rather a fight of one dog against all the rest. Gus Longstreet, who recorded "The Fox-Hunt" in his *Georgia Scenes*, said that "hounds, like the wily politicians of the present day, all jump on the undermost."

Two of the hounds, Charlie's Sounder and Squire Hicks' Buster, could be relied upon with confidence; they knew from the hour of the hunt and the equipment of the huntsmen the game they would pursue. There would be no rabbits or deer noticed today.

One of the dogs, for the first time of the day, was in a gully, rooting around, trying to conjure up a fox. After she returned to the pack and back to the gully three times, Thomson was getting bored. While waiting for the dog, his freezing limbs made him think, "*How could I have been so crazy to have thought that I would find any pleasure in this? I don't think we'll see a fox, and if we do, what are the cries of twenty or thirty hounds to three or four hours of exposure on this morning? Why didn't I bring an overcoat and some gloves on a cold, cold morning as this?*"

Thomson had not gone far before he heard groups of four or five hounds baying in all directions. The hounds had all shamefully decided to hunt for Peter Cottontail, all except Sounder and Buster. Thomson thought, "*Let them chase the rabbits. Why should we seek amusement in the tortures of a poor unoffending animal? Around this countryside, I've never heard of a single loss traced to a fox, not even of a goose, much less of a lamb. This little jaunt has broken my rest, has jeopardized my health, and has caused me suffering this morning. This is folly; this is madness, in the extreme.*"

Thomson was awakened from his revelry by the loud voice of Buster. "Hark! Listen!" Sounder joined his hunting-mate with a cry of his own. The two hounds had always hunted together and their loyalty to each other was undeniable. In a second, all the other hounds were silenced. They stopped in their tracks and then hurried to join Buster and Sounder.

Loud shrieks of joy arose from the throats of the huntsmen as they also dashed to the two favorite dogs.

Thomson watched as Epp charged right into the forest at half-speed, ignoring the branches as best he could, to take control of the pack. Thomson thought that surely he could slowly follow where Epp had tread and had plunged into darkness.

The sun had risen, but it did Thomson no good in the forest. After sixty paces, a limb swiped Thomson across his face. It came like a stroke of lightning over Thomson's frozen face. Thomson's face felt like it was covered with streaks of fire interwoven with streaks of ice.

Venturing forward, hoping the woods would end, Thomson's horse sauntered between two young saplings covered with grape-vines. Passing through, Thomson's neck was caught by one vine. His hat flew off, and about the time his hat hit the ground, Thomson's rear end did likewise.

Thomson lay there wondering, *"How did Epp Wilson fly through this forest when I could not even walk through it?"* Thomson suddenly realized what a great asset a nice, warm hat was on a cold day such as this. Thomson finally reached the edge of the woods and rejoined the huntsmen.

No encouraging sounds could be heard from the hounds, but soon the voices of the two favorites could be heard. Finally, the whole pack broke out in song. The fox was up with almost thirty foes in pursuit.

Thomson was absolutely enthralled by the events unfolding before his eyes. The fox had not wanted to leave his burrow because the hounds were right behind him when he entered the field. The huntsmen, emerging from the forest and gaining the heights around, gave a mighty roar when they caught the first glimpse of the pack.

Suddenly, all the hounds were hushed. Not a sound was heard. They were knocked out, as it was called, near the corner of the field belonging to Miss Pinkie, the hunt's matriarch. No hounds could find the scent. Epp thought that maybe the fox was playing a trick.

Epp thought that maybe the fox had climbed upon Miss Pinkie's fence and had walked down it a ways. Epp took a couple of hounds along the fence side, and after three hundred yards the dogs were reintroduced to the trail. The cry was now renewed with the same spirit in which it had begun.

Thomson came upon a large log in his path while following the cries of the hounds. He thought, *"If I can get this nag to jump over this log, I will then try to jump the first small fence we come to."* He dug his heels into the horse and it picked up a pace that Thomson thought might just clear the log.

When the old boy got close to the log, within jumping distance of it, he just stopped. He stood there is if waiting for Thomson to lower it. Thomson thought that if he wouldn't run and jump the log, he would at least stand and walk over it.

Thomson prodded the horse forward, but the nag kept going to the left or right to go around it. Finally, the horse lazily raised his forefeet and threw them over the log! He stood there without movement. Thomson waited to see if he would continue over the log on his own, but he began a backward motion as if he would fall down back where he had begun. Thomson gave him a hard kick in the flank and the old nag dragged his hind feet over.

In the meantime, the fox had crossed the path just thirty steps ahead of Thomson. Epp Wilson came roaring up on his steed and shouted, "Did you see him? Was his brush up or down?"

Thomson mumbled that as far as he could tell, it was neither, but to make a joke he said, "I didn't see either. The only brushing I saw was when it brushed beside me." Experienced fox-hunters know how tired the fox is by the manner in which he carries his tail. Thomson had no idea what Epp was asking. Disgusted, Epp spurred his steed and sped away.

The fellows had gathered at Foxboro after the hunt to enjoy a pint or two of mead and beer. Epp's servants had prepared a nice platter of pork and venison for all to enjoy with their greens and beans.

Reverend Paul, the local Methodist preacher and a non-hunting guest like Thomson, began telling one of his usually humorous stories, but being a man of the cloth, he couldn't swear to its veracity. However, he did state emphatically that it was the absolute truth.

One of his church members was noted for his skill as a marksman. According to Andy's claims, he had killed deer, wild turkeys, and other game with his rifle at such long range that it was hard to believe. The people who knew Andy found it hard to believe, but strangers never would believe it at all. Unfortunately, Andy's unbelievably fantastic feats always occurred when no one else was there to witness the performance.

The Reverend began to feel that Brother Andy's propensity to exaggerate was bringing reproach upon the church. A committee was named to visit with Andy and convince him to stop his evil ways. The preacher and the committee met at Andy's home but felt they should not discuss their church business there. Everybody moved down the road a couple of miles to a neighbor's house. Andy had no clue as to their mission, but readily agreed. On the way out of his house, he grabbed his rifle from its pegs over the mantle, just in case he saw that hawk that had been killing his chickens. They had gone about halfway to the neighbor's when Andy stopped and said, "There he is now."

"Where?" said the Reverend.

Pointing to a large poplar a long distance away, Andy replied, "Look up that tree about fifty feet and then over to the right about ten feet. He's sitting on a nest in the crook of that limb." The preacher and the committee looked and looked, but no one could see the hawk, much less the nest.

"What? Can't you see the hawk? Why, I can see his eyes." The churchmen shifted all around and strained their eyes, but it was no help. "Well, I'll show him to you." Andy raised his rifle, took a careful bead and fired. As the smoke cleared, the hawk fell to the ground with a dull thud.

An examination of the hawk showed that the ball had passed right through one of the hawk's eyes and exited the other. The men were incredulous, and the Reverend, feeling quite uncomfortable, said, "Brother Andrew, I had heard so many of your incredible stories that I had my doubts about their truth. But I've seen enough. You killed that hawk and we couldn't even see his nest. I'm going home. Please forgive my doubting you."

From that day on, no one at the church would ever doubt a thing that Andy said. When Dr. Lindley heard the story, he said, "I'm not surprised. He could see a honey bee a quarter of a mile away. Once Bob Hawes and Andy and I were passing a peach shed, and Bob said, 'Can you see that fly buzzing around the top of that shed?'"

Andy said, "No, but I can hear him buzz."

"Nobody would ever doubt it," was the final word from Dr. Lindley.

Thomson marveled at his day, but he had had his fill of fox-hunting at Foxboro. He was full and headed back to Cap' Wilson's and then to Augusta for the remainder of the weekend. He thoroughly enjoyed the great sport and would tell its story for the rest of his life. As enjoyable as Wilson's company was, Thomson had to move on, especially with the weather finally cooperating.

The following summer, while sitting at a table outside his favorite restaurant, enjoying the cool summer shade of a massive oak, Edgar Thomson listened as Gus Longstreet was speaking. "You'll never believe what I did yesterday. I was riding by Judge King's house on Broad Street on the way to buy some spicy ham that had just come in. My empty hamper basket was tied to the back of my buggy, and as I came up to the Judge's house, I found the road filled with chickens scratching in the dirt for their next meal. My mind could only focus on chicken pot pie, fried chicken and chicken salad. Suddenly it hit me; there was only one thing to do.

"I got out of the buggy, hitched my horse and yelled, 'Hey, Judge, give me a hand.'

"Judge King yelled, 'Hello, old friend, what's the problem?'

"I said, 'Judge, I've had terrible luck. I started out for the store with a basket full of chickens to sell and just as I reached the front of your place, the top blew off. All my chickens got loose right here in front of your place. Can you help me?'

"The Judge scooted around back of the house and summoned a couple of his men. I pointed out the best of the hens and the darkies loaded them into my basket. I thanked the Judge and his men and proceeded on to the store for my hams."

Old Gus Longstreet was one of the finest humorists this nation has ever seen, or read. He lived his life in humor, and he enjoyed most every minute. Judge Longstreet's mother, who lived in downtown Augusta, asked her gifted son to draw up her will. He said she had nothing to bequeath and put it off. She kept insisting and he presented her a first draft in solemn, legal form. The will bequeathed a pair of worn out shoes she kept under her bed and other items of absolutely no worth. He read it to her with a solemn face until she jumped up and said, "Get out of here, Gus. I always thought you were a silly goose, and now I know it's true."

A little later, Longstreet was standing in front of Washington Hall on the corner of Broad and McIntosh Streets, listening to Daniel Webster speak from the balcony. Webster, that great defender of the Constitution, was suffering from so much Augusta hospitality that he could not stand on his feet for any length of time. He, therefore, had to shorten his speech which made one gentleman in the audience suggest that it was "short and brief."

Another political icon of the era was Henry Clay. In 1844, Augustans were proud to say they had heard him speak downtown. He arrived an hour before he was to speak, hot and dusty and tired, for it was a scorching summer day. Retiring to one of the courthouse rooms to remove the soot and dust of the morning's travel, he returned in a few moments looking fresh, tall and erect.

For an hour or more Clay charmed the audience with his fine address. His grace, his voice, and his sharp eyes made him an unforgettable figure to behold. He was entertained while in Augusta by Mrs. Emily Tubman, who had been his ward during her girlhood days in Kentucky.

The religious faith and zeal of the early days found its fulfillment through the old camp meetings. At White Oak Campground, Fountain Campground, and Richmond Campground, the country worshipers took to the woods, God's first temple, and made their vows afresh. The social aspects of these old-time meetings brightened and relieved the dull monotony of the rural, isolated life for weeks to come.

In the early years, no "tents" were built on the campgrounds, but later, little rough shacks sprung up to house the faithful. The people came in covered wagons and these were used as sleeping quarters during the meeting. As the worshipers improved financially, they would erect and enlarge buildings to shelter their families during the services. The largest of them would house, sleep, and feed forty or fifty guests in addition to their own families.

6 Making Progress, Settlers, and Squatters

Thomson pushed himself and his men. They carefully, but quickly, tore through Mesena, Camak, Norwood, and Barnett, to Crawfordville, sixty-five miles west of Augusta, and then to Union Point and Greensboro. Extending the Athens branch, originally planned as the most important part of the line, had been put on hold, forgotten for the moment. Thomson concluded his detailed profile maps on April 14, 1835.

More than half the people living in this part of Georgia were original inhabitants, or first settlers. These people were a race of men who could not stay very long on the land upon which they settled. They were always on the move for healthier climate, finer hunting grounds, or richer soil. They continued westward to the fringes of the white man's land. They farmed or hunted there for a while and then moved on beyond the frontier and into the Indians' land. Their treatment of the Indians caused constant ill-feeling. That frequently flared into bloodshed, and the Indian was always the loser, not from a lack of courage, but from a shortage of numbers.

These settlers spent much of their time hunting deer and bears, whose meat they ate and whose skins they sold. The settlers usually spent so much time hunting that they tended to neglect their newly acquired land. They normally owned between one hundred and four hundred acres, but they cleared and cultivated only eight or ten. The crops from this land and the milk from their cows were quite sufficient for them.

Their families seldom included less than six or seven children. Their houses were usually located in a beautiful spot with a great view. It would have been hard for anyone to have a house situated otherwise. But their houses were nothing more than miserable log huts with no windows. They were so small that two beds usually took up the room. One of the huts could be built by two men in less than three days. From the small size and the sorry state of construction, no one would have believed these huts came from a forest of trees where timber could be had just for the asking.

These settlers of Georgia, as elsewhere in the States, did not object to receiving strangers. Just the opposite; visitors were like receiving mail or newspapers or family. That's how these folks got their news. They gave the strangers shelter, which meant they allowed them to sleep on the floor wrapped in blankets. They ate cornbread, smoked ham, deer and bear, milk and butter, peas and beans, but seldom anything else. Very little money was spent on food in this part of the country.

When Thomson arrived and gave his reports, the Board praised him for the excellent work and its timeliness in such weather, and authorized the letting of construction contracts for the main line from Union Point to Greensboro. In the spring, Thomson reviewed existing construction contracts, evaluated proposed contracts, and completed his surveys to Madison and to Eatonton, a branch which would never be completed.

Eatonton, a village since 1808, was named for American diplomat General William Eaton. The Connecticut-born Eaton was a hero of the First Barbary War at Tripoli and testified against Aaron Burr at his treason trial. Joel Chandler Harris, the great American humorist, was born in Eatonton, as were Uncle Remus and Brer Rabbit. In later years, Alice Walker, the author of *The Color Purple*, would also begin her life there.

Thomson recommended that the main line be extended to Madison, and the Board, quite impressed with Thomson's location, agreed to let grading contracts for twenty-five additional miles. By September 1, 1835, the Georgia Rail Road Company had fifty-four miles of track under contract to be constructed and half of its main line and branches to be surveyed.

Union Point, the place which was to be the junction of the eventual main line and the branch line to Athens, was seventy-six miles from Augusta. Thomson's field work was quickly outstretching the ability of the company to raise the necessary funds to feed the creature being made. On September 8, 1835, the Board called for another $15 per share stock installment and formed a committee to meet with state legislators to draft a bill for a state loan. James Camak had some doubts about the propriety of such a loan.

"Mr. Camak," Thomson reasoned, "you have been a driving force with this project since day one. You are a sensible, intelligent businessman. There is no reason that a legitimate company owned by stockholders such as we should not qualify for a loan. We have risked our personal money to fund a capital improvement by which the entire country will benefit. We should certainly ask our legislature for an interest-bearing loan. We have paid for all our costs to date without a dime given us by the state of Georgia or the federal government.

"All we have been given is the charter allowing us to build our road through private land, but we have compensated all landowners for those easements. We have paid and are still paying dearly for them. We will not be asking for a gift, just a loan. We would appreciate your blessing on this request."

Easements and purchased rights-of-way were necessary to establish where the tracks would be located along the proposed routes. Landowners could litigate if the compensation amount for either was in dispute, but it was time-consuming, expensive, and usually fruitless. Many times, railroad officials tried to acquire a right-of-way from someone who was not a landowner but a squatter, unbeknownst at first to the railroad officials.

These squatters were people who, without any title to the land, plopped themselves down and declared themselves the lords and masters of their soil for the time being. There was nobody to question their rights out on the frontier, and it may not have been very smart to have ever brought up the subject with them. These hardy fellows were called the pioneers of the wilderness, for they forged ahead of the more orderly and civilized population and cleared away the grounds of the line of human white surge across our continent. They were known to have no affection for the law. When the tide of population crept up to them, they took their axes and hightailed it beyond those righteous regulators of other people's affairs—judges and juries.

Old Cap' Wilson had a reputation for being quite tight with his money, but there were times when he showed his kindness. Riding over his estate one day, he chanced upon a poorer neighbor, a squatter he had taken under his wing. The neighbor had slaughtered one of Wilson's cows and was in the act of butchering it for his own use. After reprimanding the man for his theft, Cap' asked, "Have you any salt to cure it?"

"No, sir," said the man.

"Then send over to my house and I will give you what you need." Putting his spurs to his horse, he proceeded on his way.

Thomson encountered many of these squatters on the route of his railroad. Their nickname was Crackers, but they were just honest squatters, free and easy settlers, who were their own law-makers or law-breakers as the case may be. Many of these squatters remained on the land where they became useful citizens. The riff-raff, the idlers and the rovers, moved on westward.

The construction of the Georgia Rail Road was indeed legitimate and there was a great need for it. Too many businesses had a terrible problem with transporting equipment into the interior of Georgia. William Dearing explained the problem to his state representative, the newly elected Alexander Stephens, "As you know, the Savannah River at Augusta going north upstream is virtually impassable to all water traffic. Its rapids are crammed with boulders, large and small.

"The only water transportation to the upper Savannah is by canoe or those long, skinny Petersburg boats. They can't transport a thing! You have seen it for yourself. You know all this, but let me make my point. All machinery coming from England, or even New England, by water has to be unloaded in Augusta and placed on heavy, mule-drawn wagons.

"Winter rains flood all the major roads around Augusta, and those over-burdened wagons sometimes sink to their undercarriage, transforming them into platforms upon which their cargo sits. The two of them, the wagon and its cargo, are stuck there in mutual bondage in the middle of the so-called road until the beginning of spring. A couple of fine spring days will thaw out and dry up the mud, and the wagon will be dug out, and the shipment will begin anew."

The mudhole incident was printed in *The Sun and New York Herald* on April 20, 1920 and was titled "Mudhole Started Georgia Rail Road." James Camak, William Williams, Asbury Hull, and William Dearing were building the Princeton Factory in Athens. They were awaiting the arrival of an important piece of equipment sent from Savannah via Augusta by river and then to Athens by wagons pulled by teams of six mules each. It was the winter of 1832, the weather was brutal, and the equipment didn't arrive. The mudhole quagmire was the impetus for the beginning of the Georgia Rail Road.

"Oh, sure," Dearing continued, "we could build a bunch of corduroy-roads, which would help a little, but they would be expensive and would require constant maintenance. In rainy weather they would allow us to send some goods over them, but you can only travel about two or three miles an hour on them.

"Think of the expense of having four or five men at all times cutting down trees and trimming them into twelve foot logs. Then the workers have to dig out the old rotted logs and replace them with new logs of the same length and width. Why, we'd have to have twenty men in the field at all times!

"A dependable railroad will prevent this terrible waste of time and money. It will surely bring great rewards to even the smallest of hamlets, even your lovely Crawfordville. Just think, one day your beautiful Liberty Hall will be in the center of a fine, elegant city. We will remember any help you can give us in securing our loan. The future of our railroad is the future of your town."

The state charter that allowed the company to acquire the easements also exempted the company from all state and local taxes. However, the company was required to pay an annual fee of one-half of one percent of the company's net earnings to the state. That agreement was unique to Georgia, but a state charter system was the general legislative policy throughout the entire country.

The building of a new railroad was usually a necessary business venture chartered by appropriate state legislatures. However, there was a way, a scheme actually, to get rich quick by starting a new railroad. Thomson had lunch one day in Augusta with three men who said they had plenty of money and wanted to talk to him about investing it with him. The rougher looking of the three, a Mr. Guinn, started the conversation.

"Mr. Thomson, if you please, let me explain our ideas about building a new railroad with your help. We have recently been the developers of a failed railroad in Missouri. We were promoting a rail connection from St. Louis to Columbia, a little shy of one hundred miles. We were just promoting it, you know; we weren't really interested in building it. Columbia did not have a railroad and her civic leaders, so to speak, were anxious to get one.

"We organized our company with the purpose of laying rail between the two cities. Like I said, almost a hundred miles of track. Once the company was formed, we went to the Missouri legislature to get a charter and a loan of public funds. We asked for a land grant. The federal government has been discussing giving free land in the West to railroad companies. Their plan is to give the railroads six square miles of land for every mile of track they built. They're trying to populate the West.

"Well, sir, the federal government up and surprised us. They said we were to be a test case for the program. We got six square miles for every mile we were to build, just like they said. Six hundred square miles of prime Missouri real estate. Of course, we had to grease a few palms, but what can you expect in today's world? We showed our brightly colored maps of our land holdings to wealthy potential investors all over the East and in Europe. Since our railroad owned such a large tract of land, the people knew we could not fail. Fortunately, that was not true. Fortunately for us, that is, but unfortunately for them.

"After the railroad was built, we sold this land to a legitimate real estate syndicate for a dollar and a quarter an acre. They were happy with the deal; they sold it for two dollars and a half an acre to the new settlers arriving by the railroad or a wagon train. Everybody was happy. We milked those fools dry. Once we pulled out all the capital, we bankrupted the railroad and sold it for ten cents on the dollar. Yes, sir, we're all mighty millionaires now. We want to do it again, but our reputations, so to speak, are not the best at present."

Mr. Guinn finally came to the point. "So we need a man like you, Mr. Thomson, to join with us and pull off another beautiful scheme, so to speak. We're just humble millionaires who will keep out of the public view, you know, and let all the light shine on you. We know you're one of the highest-paid engineers in the country, but, Mr. Thomson, that's peanuts compared to what we can offer you."

Thomson exploded, "My God, man, what makes you think I'd even consider such a thing? You miscreants must excuse me, I'm sorry but I think I'm going to get sick. Get out of my office, and stay out!"

The Georgia Rail Road, in the competent hands of Edgar Thomson and his directors, would have no such fate. But not everyone connected with the company believed that. At the stockholders' meeting in May of 1835, one stockholder, Henry Potter, stood up and said, "I hate to complain, but the exorbitant salaries being paid to our engineers are going to bankrupt this company. Mr. Thomson makes twice what our president makes and is paid as much as any chief engineer in the country. Can he and his overpaid fellow engineers be worth what we're paying them?"

William Williams answered the question, "Everyone at this meeting knows that money is tight, and expenses are enormous, but they are absolutely necessary. We are dealing with the building of a railroad. We all knew what the costs would be from the beginning. Mr. Thomson has done a great job and I believe he fully deserves every penny he makes.

"I know there's a feeling of panic in the air throughout this whole country. I know the economy is terrible, but we must trust in Mr. Thomson to complete our road, on schedule and within our budget. Who could we ever find to take his place?" A resolution was passed that the salaries paid Thomson and his hand-picked engineers were justified at that time.

In October of 1835, the Board met to discuss asking the state for banking privileges for the company. "We need a vehicle to get our name out into the market place. We must become better known to investors if we are going to be able to raise the necessary funds to build this road. We need to become a bank as well as a railroad."

The state legislature granted the company banking privileges and officially changed its name to Georgia Rail Road and Banking Company on December 18, 1835. The scope of the entire enterprise was stated in the preamble to the amended charter. "The people of the West have in contemplation to make a communication between the city of Cincinnati and the Southern Atlantic coast by means of a railroad." An integral link of that connection would be the Georgia Rail Road.

The principal bank of the newly redesigned company was located in Athens, the company's original base. Athens was home to about seven hundred people in the mid-1830s. James Camak resigned as President, Treasurer, and General Agent of the Company to become the Cashier of the Athens bank. A lot was purchased and the Augusta banking house was soon opened. Company officials and the public quickly began to use the word "Railroad," instead of the old fashioned "Rail Road" on their correspondence. Eventually another change would take place; the company would move to Augusta, and the Athens bank branch would close.

The capital stock of the company was specified not to exceed two million dollars. Not more than half of that could be used for banking purposes until the railroad was completed. The shareholders immediately called for an additional 7,500 shares of stock to be authorized and issued. Excitement was in the air. The new company's stock soared due to the directors' financial expertise in funding the company and to Edgar Thomson's engineering ability in getting the railroad constructed. The new subscriptions exceeded the offering on the first day. Individuals put ads in their local papers trying to find shares to buy. Shares traded at an average of a ten percent premium.

During the March quarterly Board meeting, Thomson was asked to report on his efforts in purchasing the railroad's rolling stock. "Gentlemen, I have made some major moves concerning the acquisition of our first locomotives. As you know, I do not want our competitors to know our immediate plans, so I have quietly ordered seven locomotives from my Philadelphia friend, Matthias Baldwin. We need to keep this a secret, even from the stockholders, at this time. I ordered the distance between the drivers on the locomotives at five feet to agree to the Charleston & Hamburg Railroad. Once we build a bridge across the Savannah, Charleston will be directly connected to us and westward to the interior of the state."

Matthias Baldwin was an inventor and a manufacturer of the finest locomotives in the world. He built his first experimental steam locomotive in 1831. It was unusual; it burned coal, which was readily available in the North, and not wood. He established the Baldwin Locomotive Works in Philadelphia, and it became one of the largest and most successful locomotive manufacturers in America.

"Edgar, you really should revisit your stand on slavery," Matt once told Thomson. "I get great pleasure and personal pride in being an abolitionist. Our work has just begun. One day we foresee this country as being free of all slaves. The whole country, not just the North. I've even put my money where my mouth, I guess I should say heart, is. I've set up a free school for the blacks in Philadelphia. When the public funds for operations run out, I'm going to pay the teachers' wages from my own pocket."

Baldwin's competitors, all in the North, sent their representatives throughout the South, trying to use his activities on behalf of the abolitionists against him. Thomson answered Matt's challenge, "I do not care about your views on that sorry system. I don't really care how any of you people think about it. I have no strong feelings about it myself, one way or the other. All I want from you, dear Baldwin, are the best locomotives that your company can make and my money can buy."

Thomson also retained a firm in Philadelphia to acquire iron for him. A majority of the original contractors on the road were also Philadelphia companies. William Dearing took Thomson aside during a Board meeting and said, "Mr. Thomson, you have utilized the services of your Philadelphia friends almost exclusively. Are there no businesses in Georgia good enough that we can patronize them to establish good future business relations? I looked at your labor invoices the other day and all of your expenditures for the salaries and subsistence of your laborers indicate that they, too, are from elsewhere."

Edgar leaned towards the director he felt closest to and said with conviction, "Mr. Dearing, most of our laborers are indeed Europeans. They're almost all Irish Catholics. They left their homes to come to this country for a better life. They get off their boats, they need jobs, and my agents send them down here. They left their families in Ireland; working is the only thing they have to do here. They do drink when it's available, but they are a lot less trouble to me than working with any of these locals, black or white."

William E. Dearing, born in 1785 in Culpepper County, Virginia, immigrated to Washington, Georgia as a young man and established himself as a respected businessman. Washington was settled in 1773 by Stephen Heard who named the town for his Virginia neighbor, George Washington. This was the first town to be named after our first president, the first Southern town to have a cotton mill, the first to have a Southern woman newspaper editor, and the first to hang a woman.

Dearing became partners with John Cormick who had purchased

the business of Luis Prudhomme, a French merchant and slave trader. In 1812, the firm of William Dearing and Company became the first of many lucrative businesses Dearing ventured into in real estate, banking, merchandising, and in the development of the Georgia Rail Road. Later, as President of the railroad, Dearing maintained a residence in Augusta, as did John Cormick.

Dearing and his company had invested heavily in the first cotton mill south of Connecticut. The company produced woolen and cotton goods by machinery but was unable to cope with its financial and production burdens and closed in 1816. In 1818, Dearing built a three-story brick structure on the corner of Main and Spring Streets in Washington, where he maintained his office until 1825.

The year 1836 had been a great year for the railroad and the country, surely the country's most exciting event of the year occurred when Texas broke away from Mexico. Texas' swarms of settlers, adventurers, and land speculators formed a Texas Republic under Andrew Jackson's old friend Sam Houston. For a time it appeared there would neither be a Texas nor a Houston. Surging north from Mexico to recover the land taken by the new Texans, as they proudly called themselves, General Santa Anna's seven thousand men annihilated the tiny Alamo garrison.

Sam Houston, with a greatly inferior force, managed to surprise and overwhelm the Mexicans at the San Jacinto River and captured Santa Anna. The national excitement was unbelievable. John C. Calhoun pushed immediately to recognize the new republic and to admit it into the Union. He and his fellow Southerners looked to Texas as a new slave state, giving them an edge in electoral voting. Andrew Jackson would not support Calhoun's resolutions because it was right before an election, and he didn't want to upset his party's chances at the polls in the North.

In 1836, Texas was as far west as most Americans could get their heads around. California was still a feudal backwater between the sea and the mountains. It was populated by proud families of Spanish blood, called Californios. Their courtly life was sustained by the labor of the gentle Indians living there. Occasionally, white men would come into the sunny valleys from their cabins in the mountains. They scared the Californios to death. They were rough and hard-drinking but fortunately they were few in number. By 1836, there were only two hundred foreigners, mostly Americans, living in California.

Among them was a Swiss adventurer, John Sutter, who had gone bankrupt as a dry-goods merchant and had left his wife and children and fled across the Atlantic. He followed a band of trappers to Oregon, sailed from Hawaii to Alaska, and settled in California. Sutter lived in the empty Sacramento Valley as a Mexican citizen on fifty-thousand acres of land granted him by the Mexican Governor. In the mid-1840s Sutter's land would be overwhelmed by the influx of the Gold Rushers, who were drawn like a magnet to the newly discovered gold fields on Sutter's land.

Relishing the national news, Thomson was very excited and optimistic about the future. He began encouraging his directors to push for expansion to make the Georgia Railroad a vital link in the first connection between the Atlantic Ocean and the Mississippi River. Trying to bring to reality these oft dreamed-of connections to the Mississippi River, Thomson spent much of his summer locating a line from Athens to Knoxville and another line from Athens to the proposed Hiawassee Railroad. Thomson's railroad was not going to be the entire chain connecting the Atlantic Ocean to the Mississippi River; it was going to be only a link in the chain. That would be enough at the present.

Meeting for lunch at the Richmond Hotel, Thomson and his good friend Gus Longstreet raved over the possible annexation of Texas to the Union. Thomson talked about building a railroad out there, and connecting it to a railroad he would one day build from Georgia to the Mississippi River. Longstreet, when it became his turn to talk, shared a recent personal experience with Thomson.

In 1834, Longstreet found the time to establish his own newspaper, the *Augusta State Rights' Sentinel*. He put most of his stories in print in the daily papers all over Georgia, but had not yet written this one. The contents of his newspaper showed his conservative, constitutional, state rights views.

Longstreet had been invited to a dance party given at the Old Government House by an old classmate from Richmond Academy. "I had only decided to go in hopes of seeing an old flame of mine," he told Thomson. "I was hoping she had married someone who was at the dance. My old buddy Danny Hammond had come to town on business and we went together without our wives.

"We talked awhile and listened to some Negroes playing their fiddles. The other guests were arriving, but I didn't see my old girlfriend, Jeannie Brooks. I got tired of looking and started asking the other guests if any of them knew her. To my surprise, I met her husband.

"He told me she was in the kitchen helping prepare the food. He offered to take me to her, but I said I would wait 'til the dancing began and surprise her myself. I knew she would just swoon when she saw me again.

"I stayed out of her way until the dancing started, and then I walked up to her as she sat on a bench resting from her efforts with the food. I held my hand out and she took it. I asked her to dance and she replied she never danced. I asked her again, but she said, 'No, but thanks just the same.'

"I said, don't you know who I am? She said she could not remember ever seeing me before. I went through a litany of friends we had shared. Oh, she said, she remembered every one of them, but she could not remember me at all.

"I finally got mad and had had enough. I retired from her side without a word goodbye, and Danny and I went to the Hotel bar for a drink. The whole incident ruined my night, although being with Danny again made it all worthwhile.

"Danny was always full of high jinx. He played the fool everywhere he went. The next day, we were at the market, and he engaged a poor old Negro woman to sell him one half of a living chicken. Do sell it to me, he begged, my wife is very sick, and is longing for some chicken pie.

"This is all the money I have," he said as he set down one half the price of the whole chicken.

"No, massa. How I gwine cut live chicken in two?"

"I don't want you to cut it in two while it's alive. I want you to kill it, clean it, and then divide it."

"Name of God! What sort o' chance I got to clean chicken in the market-house. Whay de water fo to scall um and wash um?"

"Don't scald it at all; just pick it."

"Bess be to God! De fedders fly all ober de place and de bucherman's meat. He come bang me fo sure. No, massa, I mighty sorry fo your wife, but I no cutty chicken open."

7 Fruitland, Corporate Slavery, and The Financial Panic Of 1837

By the end of 1836, the Georgia Railroad had seventy-six miles of rail to Union Point under contract. Thomson approached the Board and declared, "I am ready to start work on the Athens branch. Gentlemen, I have determined that laying the thirty-six mile road from Union Point to Athens will cost $10,287 per mile. I'm positive that is accurate. You may, therefore, need to make a provision for around $370,000 to pay for it, depending upon where we finally place the terminal. There is a soil and water problem to be worked out."

William Dearing made the motion, "To raise the necessary $370,000 to complete the proposed branch to Athens, I move that the Board call for another cash installment of subscribed stock to be paid in and for another 3,000 shares of company securities to be sold. This motion should not concern our investors because they are happy; those who had originally paid $65 for a share of company stock can now sell them for $87 each in Augusta."

The directors soon found that the company's banking business was an important source of funds. Eighty percent of the Board's time was now spent exclusively for banking concerns. Thomson was delighted; this gave him a free hand to continue his own work without interference from them, or even having to meet with them. The Board raised Edgar's salary to $4,000 a year, effective in November.

By the middle of 1836, the company was faced with several problems. Meeting with the stockholders, Thomson reported, "The project is going well; I hear our finances are satisfactory, and the company still has a very bright future. I have reviewed our progress report and our expenditures to date. I have also re-estimated the costs of building our road based on these figures plus the expected inflation of them in the near future. The result is that our new estimated cost of construction is $5,230 per mile.

"However, our major problems, as you all know, are this chronic inflation throughout the country and a severe shortage of labor around here in particular. Almost all white laborers have fled from the South to accept higher paying wages up North. I don't blame them, but it's ruining our construction schedule. The lack of available laborers, particularly after June 1st, has caused the total suspension of work on the line."

It was not until the fall that enough workers had been rehired so that grading work could continue on to Crawfordville, a tiny town then just as it is today. Crawfordville, named for William Harris Crawford, the great American statesman, was the birthplace and home of Alexander Stephens. Stephens, a brilliant young lawyer practicing in town, certainly befriended Thomson. Thomson would reciprocate the friendship by contributing to Stephens' political ambitions, which would lead him to the Vice Presidency of the Confederacy. In the winter, very wet and very cold weather once again delayed progress until the spring of 1837.

The spiral in wages during 1836 and 1837 caused many construction companies to forfeit their contracts which had been negotiated earlier when the price of labor and supplies was much lower. Thomson told his road engineer, "We are going to have to resort to using local contractors to complete this defaulted work. The majority of these local contractors are using slave labor, especially during the off season. Just get used to it. You can't change anything."

After the fields had been planted and before the harvest, and during the winter, most field hands were just barely kept busy. Their owners were anxious to rent them out to companies requiring their manual labor. They were the perfect answer to the labor problem.

Thomson's attitude towards slavery could not have been demonstrated better than by his next actions. He asked for a meeting with the Board in Athens. "Once again, gentlemen, I need to seek your personal guidance and your business opinions—this time about the company purchasing slaves to be worked on the line."

Thomson was getting along fine with the Board and saw no reason to upset the apple cart. He thought the matter of the slaves warranted getting a complete picture of how the company wanted to be seen by the rest of the country. Otherwise, he would have already bought them. He made his pitch.

"Gentlemen, will each of you be satisfied if our company would become known as an owner of slaves? Or would you rather we, as a company, be remembered as an institution that supported free men? If any slaves were ever purchased by us, and it became known to the public, how would you feel?

"I know it matters little in Georgia, but what if such an act were consummated and it becomes known to the rest of the country? I, myself, have no qualms about buying slaves, or I wouldn't have considered the idea at all, but what are we to make of your feelings?

"I recall the first time I saw slaves at auction soon after arriving in Augusta. I was surprised when I found out Augusta had two slave markets; one at both ends of Broad Street. I thought, in spite of myself, I would not be able to look at those poor souls without feelings of pity. I felt a sadness for what I thought they were going through and their unfortunate future.

"I had seen slaves before coming down south, but I was surprised that many in Augusta were happy and laughing. I felt troubled at going to the auction there in the middle of town, in the middle of the day at the slave-market, because I didn't want anyone to see me and think that I approved of it.

"I prepared myself for what, in my mind, was going to be the sale of countless miserable naked captives. I wondered what terrible scenes of inhumanity would meet my eyes, what screams of children would assault my ears. Wives would be torn from their husbands, mothers torn from their children, each to never be seen again by their loved ones.

"In the midst of the crowd I saw several well-dressed Negro men, laughing and joking with each other. I wanted to grab them and shake them until they showed some respect in sympathy for the soon to be auctioned slaves. I kept waiting for the slaves to appear, but I soon learned that the only slaves being sold that day were the same Negroes whom I had been blaming for their lack of sympathy. I saw pride in the faces of those men who had been purchased at the highest prices, and the utter despair of those who were shamed because they brought much less."

In his autobiography, Frederick Douglas wrote of how gentrified the well-treated slaves that he knew during his captivity had become. "Behind the tall-backed and elaborately wrought chairs stood the servants, fifteen in number, carefully selected, not only with a view to their capacity and adeptness, but with especial regard to their personal appearance, their graceful agility, and pleasing address.

"These servants constituted a sort of black aristocracy. They resembled the field hands in nothing except their color, and in this they held the advantage of a velvet-like glossiness, rich and beautiful. The hair, too, showed the same advantage.

"The delicately-formed colored maid rustled in the scarcely-worn silk of her young mistress, while the servant men were equally well attired from the over-flowing wardrobe of their young masters, so that in dress, as well as in form and feature, in manner and speech, in tastes and habits, the distance between these favored few and the sorrow and hunger-smitten multitudes of the quarter and the field was immense."

Thomson summed up his request. "I've turned that auction over in my mind quite a lot since then, gentlemen, and I realize that I was sent here to do a job, and it's a full-time job. I'll just have to rely on the good Lord to correct anything He sees that needs to be corrected.

"I now have no qualms, at all, over our company using these unfortunate slaves to labor on our tracks, as long as they are treated fairly and as men. I don't care what others may think; I need those men." Permission was unanimously given to Thomson by the Board to purchase seventy-two male slaves. Edgar Thomson, possibly without thinking it through, had become a de facto slave-owner.

Thomson was asked by Mr. Camak, "Thomson, dear friend, how can you talk of brotherly love and slavery at the same time, referring to the same man? Are you not your brother's keeper?"

Thomson smiled and said, "I understood that anyone who has purchased an asset, and has carefully preserved it, does not wish that anything detrimental to its future occur. The admired and loved item might be a fine horse, a fine carriage, a fine house, a painting, or a valued slave. You probably have no problem with my saying I love an inanimate object, but you ask how can I love and yet enslave a human being?

"This system cannot be changed. Just as these local planters, always the landowners, are concerned about any harsh treatment of their bonded men, I will be, too. They are not going to let someone harm their slaves in any way and will not allow them to work for any contractors who have reputations for mistreatment. I wouldn't either, but I do not have the time, or energy, to fight the system. I've lived around slaves in Pennsylvania my whole life."

Thomson was rightfully concerned about the planters' opinions. As he began to let construction contracts above Crawfordville, he had to use a contractor who had previously had such a reputation for abuse. Thomson took out advertisements in the surrounding newspapers in which he discussed the concerns of the planters. He appealed to the planters that all contractors he would use would have to assure him that all bonded laborers would be treated humanely and would merit the complete satisfaction of their owners. His endorsement of his contractors calmed the planters, and within thirty days the company hired 200 slaves for $15 per month plus subsistence.

Thomson told William Williams, "I have taken the necessary steps required to solve, for the moment, our labor shortage. The other major problem facing our company is this damned spiraling inflation. Excuse me, please forgive my language.

"The cost of iron has soared; the price of timber has gone through the roof. There is nothing I can do about the iron, but I just entered into a long-term contract with a local saw mill owner. That will give us a stable, but temporary, supply of timber and will offset its rising cost. Then, to insure an adequate supply in the future, I'm going to ask the Board to buy a saw mill for the company. I've also just finished the construction of a factory to make our rail cars. We've also completed an iron and brass factory where we'll make locomotive repairs."

Using the high cost of labor as an excuse, Thomson delayed the start of construction on the Athens branch until the end of 1837. He told the company's stockholders that he anticipated a drop in labor costs by then which would make the Athens' labor contracts much more advantageous than at present.

With all the obstacles to overcome, it was a great feat that the first ten miles of the railroad was opened on May 2, 1837. *Georgia*, one of the Baldwin locomotives, left the Augusta depot heading west. She was the first steam locomotive to pull a railroad car in Georgia. She certainly couldn't have headed east; the road began in Augusta, the eastern border of the state.

Georgia flew with great speed down the main road; the same road upon which she would soon be delivering her daily cargo of passengers and merchandise. She roared through Harrisonville, the first depot out of Augusta, with bells and whistles blaring, and she continued non-stop on to Bel Air, the second station. Thomson had prepared a small ceremony there for this opening of the first ten miles. A much larger ceremony would follow far down the road in a few years.

As *Georgia* passed through this beautiful countryside, Thomson recalled that he had almost decided to put this first ten miles of track in a different setting. It was in the midst of some magnificent flat land lightly bumped with a few gentle hills lying along the Savannah River. Two years earlier, while discussing the lay of this piece of land with one of his engineers, Thomson turned to see a finely dressed young man approaching him on horseback. "How do you do? Mr. Thomson, I presume? My name is Dennis Redmond and this is my land you're passing through."

"Good morning, Mr. Redmond. A beautiful stretch of land you have, indeed. I've done everything I can to try to keep our road away from your plantation. But I think the costs would be prohibitive to put our road along the river and that far north of my desired route. If I'm not mistaken, this tract of land was owned originally by my old friend and colleague, Judge Benjamin Warren."

"Yes, sir, that's correct. Judge Warren sold me his entire 315-acre spread. I'm going to grow peaches, apples, grapes, trees, and bushes all over it. It will be a glorious sight to see when we're finished. I will certainly appreciate anything that you can do, sir, to keep your iron horses from my plantation. Mr. Thomson, I have worked hard to develop this place into one of the finest homesteads in the country. You know, I'm an Irishman by birth and I've noticed that most of your workers are my countrymen. Lovely place, Ireland. Lovely, strong, hard-working men."

"I've heard your name in town. You're the owner of the *Southern Cultivator*. So what are you doing way out here, Mr. Redmond?"

"I am a horticulturalist by education and now by trade. This plantation I call Fruitlands. It is my short life's work to date, but with editing the paper and my other business interests in town, I find I haven't as much time as I need here to do it justice. I've been in correspondence with another horticulturalist, this one from Belgium, a Mr. Berckmans. He and his son want to buy it some day and make it into a nursery where they can develop plants of every type and description from many different countries."

"Well, I can certainly see why they like it," Thomson replied. "If I were not at the beginning of building this railroad, I would consider buying it myself. I could use it as an investment or a place to retire when this job is finished. I don't have a house anywhere. I just rent a room in Augusta and only spend my money on food and clothes. I don't have time to socialize or travel. I don't even have a lady friend. So, I may talk with you later. Good day, it's been my pleasure, but this road waits for no man. I will consider putting my line farther south of here, maybe near Bell Air. If you need me, please catch me down the line or in Augusta."

Four more of the seven Baldwin locomotives Thomson had ordered were delivered by May, 1838. The main features of the individual locomotives were a horizontal boiler, one pair of driving wheels, and a funnel smokestack adapted to cheap wood burning down south. These were the prototypes of the locomotive that became the standard of the 19th and early 20th centuries in America.

The six engines delivered by 1838 were named *Georgia, Florida, Tennessee, Kentucky, Louisiana,* and *Pennsylvania,* the latter in honor of Edgar Thomson's home state. The total cost of these was $46,500, and three larger ones were ordered. Only one of these locomotives would serve the Confederacy during the Civil War; the rest had been scrapped. *Georgia* was the Confederate participant chasing the Andrews' Raiders in Marietta in the Great Locomotive Chase.

Other locomotives delivered in 1839 were given similar names: *Mississippi, J. E. Thomson, Dr. William E. Dearing, Alabama,* and *Virginia.* In 1840, William Cumming and James Camak were honored by having locomotives named for them. Judge John King, Matt Baldwin, Richard Peters, and Lemuel Grant would follow in the next few years.

These beautiful locomotives were pampered by their owners and operators. They were washed every morning and were female in nature; they were always referred to as "she," and never as "he." They were smothered with affection. And yet these magnificent creatures weighed in at around 9,500 pounds each of wood, steel, iron, water, fuel, and fire. They could make around twenty-eight miles per hour on just their two rail tracks with a top surface area of only two inches each.

The locomotive engineers and the conductors relished the engines' special smell of hot oil and steam, especially in rainy or snowy weather. It could not have been too unpleasant because some of those men were required to work sixteen hours a day, seven days a week, for years on end. The engineers said the locomotives talked to you. They made breathing sounds, screeching, clanging, banging, hissing, and all the other sounds of vigorous life. They spoke to you through their smokestack exhaust and their steam whistles.

The engineers and conductors had seen too many things to be mesmerized into thinking that nothing dangerous lurked inside that beautiful body. The combination of her strength and speed was a disaster just waiting to happen. She could turn violent in a second as she flew down the line. She could become a killer; she could not stop, not physically stop, in time to keep from crushing some sleeping or daydreaming man or animal on her tracks. She had not been equipped with decent brakes, or even safety brakes, at this time.

The locomotive engineer became her partner in crime. Seeing anything on the tracks, he would blow the whistle and set the brakes, but it was usually too little, too late. Trains couldn't come to a screeching halt. Her engineers could never forget the faces of the helpless, or hopeless, people she killed.

In 1836, the Georgia General Assembly authorized a state-owned railroad, the Western & Atlantic Railway, from present day Atlanta to the Tennessee line near Chattanooga. Thomson saw that the southeastern end of the W&A would be only 75 miles from Madison. He drew up the plans and on Christmas Day of 1837, the Governor authorized the extension of Thomson's road beyond Madison, through Covington, to connect with the W&A terminal at the Chattahoochee River.

By year's end in 1837, Thomson had fifty miles of the road opened from Augusta to twelve miles west of the little hamlet of Thomson, Georgia, named in his honor. From this terminal near Norwood, private stage lines moved passengers and freight to Athens, Greensboro, Gainesville, and Washington, Georgia. The fact that so much progress was made by Thomson and the railroad during 1837 was a testament to his expertise.

The Panic of 1837 was a terrible financial crisis which caused a major recession. In 1832, President Andrew Jackson had vetoed the bill to re-charter the Second Bank of the United States. His supporters thought national banks gave too much preferential treatment to the rich and catered to special interest groups. They went so far as to accuse the bank administrators of using public funds to defeat Jackson in the 1828 election. Jackson removed Federal deposits, or reserves, from the national bank and placed them in state banks. This was done to undermine the effectiveness of the Second Bank whose charter ran through 1836. Jackson thought this would halt the ruinous speculation in public land and would slow the country's spiraling inflation. It brought disaster instead.

The state banks receiving reserves were called "pet banks" and were primarily in the West. The movement of such a vast amount of hard money, or coins, out west left shortages in the East. Jackson then issued his Specie Circular in July which permitted public land to be purchased only with hard money or "specie," which was what gold and silver coins were called. That circular caused a western, and then a national, real estate collapse because few people had enough specie to buy land. Commercial paper money issued by state or local banks could not be used.

The Bank of England raised its interest rates in 1836 from three to five percent. Major banks in the U. S. had to follow suit because of the global economic system then in place. New York banks scaled back on their lending, and money became very scarce. This, along with the real estate crash in the West, was the ultimate cause of the Panic of 1837. The East was hit hard, but the old South was hit the hardest. Florida and Georgia felt the strain after Louisiana, Mississippi, and Alabama. The Cotton Belt suffered the worst.

By 1837, there were few coins in Georgia, but Floridians still had enough to pay their bills through 1839. Merchants resorted to printing their own pennies, called tokens, to be used in trade. They were mostly copper, but some were brass or silver, and the size of a cent. They were accepted just as well as if the U. S. mint had made them. They were rightly called "Hard-times tokens."

Out of 850 banks in the U. S. at that time, 343 closed permanently. Another sixty-two suffered partial failures. During this downward spiral in the South, cotton prices fell. Planters took out loans to plant their crops, but with the price of cotton down, many had great losses and couldn't repay those loans. Banks failed. Farms were lost.

William Dearing said that the people of Georgia were living through times they had never seen before and times which they could not understand or manage. Dearing said that the farmers and businessmen of Georgia were the moving forces of the railroad, thus the Georgia Railroad and Banking Company had to be lenient and not foreclose on its customers. As a solution, the bank rationed the money of its depositors according to their needs rather than closing their doors as other banks had done.

This is a portrait of John Edgar Thomson with a facsimile of his autograph. Circa 1870.

THE
JOHN EDGAR THOMSON
FOUNDATION

Trustees of the Estate of
J. EDGAR THOMSON

Carl L. Rugart, Jr.
H. William Brady
John J. Haslett, II

This is a brochure of the John Edgar Thomson Foundation in Philadelphia in 1998. It is still helping young ladies today.

J. EDGAR THOMSON, THE GEORGIA RAIL ROAD YEARS, 1833 – 1845

Edgar Thomson built the Horseshoe Bend in Altoona, PA which allowed the railroad to run from Philadelphia to Pittsburgh without a great detour.

Andrew Carnegie, Thomson's best friend, built the Edgar Thomson Steel Works in Braddock, PA and named it for Thomson to get him to run it. Thomson didn't have time. This company became the U. S. Steel Corporation of today.

These steamboats are at Augusta on the Savannah River with the covered Hamburg Bridge in the distance. Circa 1905.

The headwaters of the Augusta Canal on the Savannah River provided water power to the mills in Augusta. Thomson built the canal in 1845. Circa 1908

The Sibley Cotton Mill with the Confederate Powder Works chimney saved as a memorial of the late war. Circa 1903.

Meadow Gardens, the home of Declaration signer George Walton, in a delapidated condition. Its beauty has been restored by the GA Society of the DAR. Circa 1903.

The Georgia Railroad and Banking Company building on Broad Street in Augusta. Circa 1905.

The Medical College building in Augusta circa 1903.

The old Slave Market on Broad Street in Augusta where Thomson attended some auctions. Circa 1905.

The new City Hall in Augusta circa 1903.

The Union Passenger Station was the Georgia Rail Road's Augusta depot. Circa 1903.

The King Mill in Augusta was powered like all the other manufacturers by the water rushing down the canal. Circa 1908.

The steamboat "Marian" on the Savannah River across from Hamburg with the Hamburg Bridge in the background. Circa 1905.

The United States Military Arsenal in Augusta. Circa 1903.

Accent on art. No cab to boast about, this Georgia freight locomotive was delivered in the late 1830s complete to oil-painted torchbearer on sandbox. Baldwin listed her as "plan D"

The Baldwin locomotive delivered to the Georgia Rail Road circa 1838.

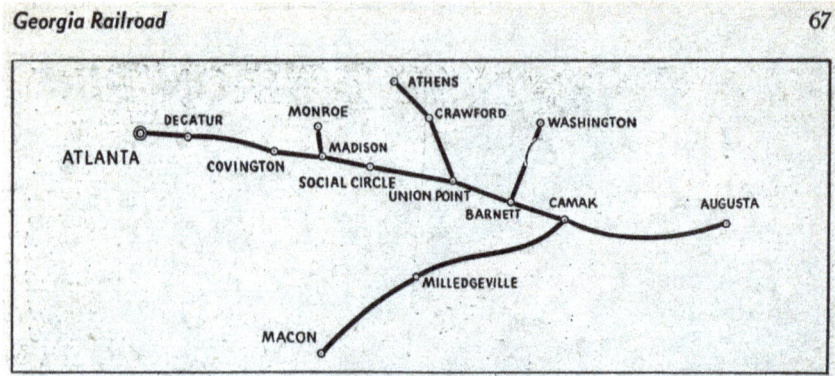

Georgia Railroad: 317 miles of trackage, including the 10.5-mile, freight-only Monroe Branch

An 1845 map of the Georgia Rail Road from Augusta to Atlanta with its connecting lines to Macon, Washington, Athens, and Monroe.

This is a unique circa 1837 ticket allowing the purchaser to travel one mile for five cents on the Georgia Rail Road. Edgar Thomson may have actually designed or approved the design of this ticket.

Edgar Thomson's personal railroad pass from the Central Ohio Rail Road for 1860.

Edgar Thomson's personal railroad pass from the New York Central Rail Road for 1860.

Edgar Thomson's personal railroad pass from the Memphis and Ohio Rail Road for 1860.

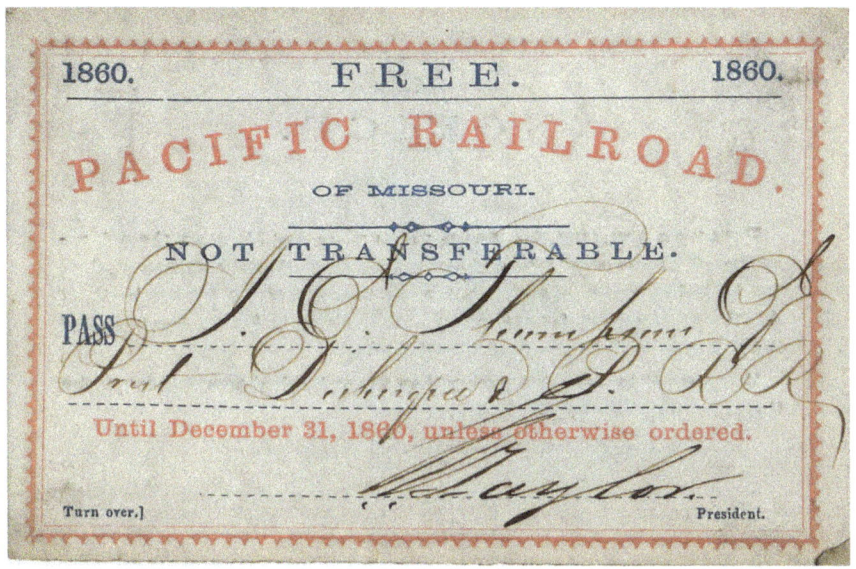

Edgar Thomson's personal railroad pass from the Pacific Rail Road for 1860.

An 1842 Georgia Rail Road and Banking Company stock certificate signed by James Camak as Cashier and John King as President.

A ten-dollar bill issued by the Bank of Augusta in 1836.

A fifty-dollar bill issued by the Bank of Hamburg in 1837.

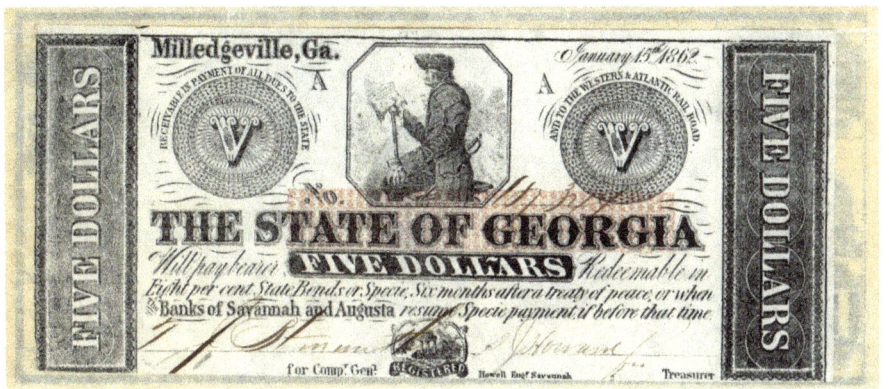

A one-dollar bill issued by the State of Georgia in 1862.

A five-dollar bill printed by the Philadelphia and Reading Rail Road Company but not issued. Circa 1830.

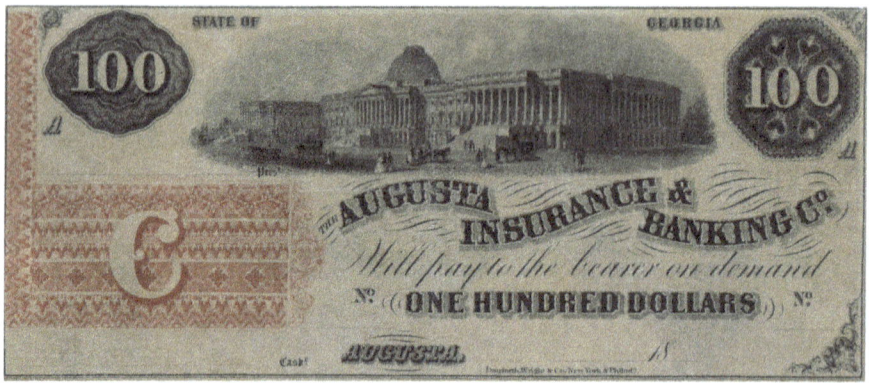

A one hundred dollar bill printed by the Augusta Insurance and Banking Company circa 1830.

A twenty dollar bill issued in 1816 by the Bridge Company of Augusta signed by Henry Shultz, its President and the founder of Hamburg, SC.

8 Money Problems and The Yellow Fever Epidemic

The Georgia Railroad directors were smart men who had been following the direction in which the country was going. They were fearful not only for the future of their railroad, but also for their country. In February of 1837, they decided not to obligate the company to any further debt. On May 17th, the bank suspended trading in specie and asked Edgar Thomson to meet with them.

"Mr. Thomson, with the uncertainty of the effects of the current financial crisis upon the future of our company, we are of the opinion that a company-wide austerity program be initiated. We, the directors of the company, wish to inquire of you your recommendation as to whether suspension of the work of the road is advisable."

Thomson sat quietly for a minute. He was caught off guard by the question. Who could imagine suspending the work on the road for any reason? "Gentlemen, I propose to you that we have come too far, too quickly, through too many trying moments, to reduce our pace now," Thomson replied.

"Thank you, Mr. Thomson, for your honesty. We expected that answer. You have always been the visionary in our group, but, sir, we have become exhausted and depressed by the magnitude of the remaining costs ahead to expand our road as we contemplated just a year ago. We have agreed beforehand to continue with your expected recommendation, but until the economy gets more stable, we will have to insist that you submit your accounts to an audit committee named by this Board.

"We will also insist on authorizing Mr. Dearing to purchase all future iron shipments for the company." William Dearing had succeeded James Camak as president of the company a year earlier. The iron purchases had been Thomson's responsibility, and he didn't particularly like the new arrangements.

The tight money and grinding inflation during the 1837 panic caused several railroads that were being considered as connecting links in the western expansion of the Georgia Railroad to fail. As much as that dour outlook cooled Thomson's vision of northern and western expansion, it crushed the enthusiasm of his directors. Thomson told his Board that the company would need at least $500,000 during 1838 to continue construction. On January 2, 1838, William Dearing was reluctantly authorized to borrow that amount.

"Ladies and gentlemen," Thomson addressed the company's stockholders in May, 1838, "it is my pleasure to announce to you that our main line became operational to the Camak station forty-seven miles from Augusta on January 22nd of this year. I am just as pleased to assure you that within the next month Crawfordville, sixty-five miles from Augusta, will also be operational.

"And, if you would indulge me for a moment, I would like to introduce to you a personal friend of mine and a friend of our railroad, the Honorable Alexander Stephens from Crawfordville. He is in town for a state legislature meeting and agreed to come with me so I could brag on him. Representative Stephens has been instrumental in assisting us in the quick culmination of contract and right-of-way disputes these last few months."

As Thomson swept his arm towards a frail, sickly looking, tiny piece of man sitting almost hidden on the front row of seats, he concluded, "He is an excellent lawyer and a fine politician. I hear he'll go far in the political arena; today a state representative, tomorrow a state senator, and then a U. S. Senator. Who knows? Maybe one day he'll be the President or the Vice President of this country."

On March 27, 1838, citizens from Wilkes County met at their Courthouse Square and elected five delegates to go to Athens and meet with the directors of the Georgia Railroad; it would be fifteen years before the requested branch railroad would be a reality.

At the annual stockholders' meeting in May, 1839, Thomson proudly reported that the main line was open to Jefferson Hall, two miles short of Union Point and seventy-four miles from Augusta. He also reported that iron had been laid almost to the Greensboro depot ten miles farther up the road. He then made the most important request of his tenure with the railroad.

"Ladies and gentlemen, I believe that we have now come face to face with the most important decision in the company's short history. Now is not the time to be timid in our work. Let us move forward with the extension of our main line and connect it with the approved state road which will begin in Chattanooga and end at the Chattahoochee River. Let us move forward with our own road from Augusta to the Chattahoochee, to the place they call Terminus. Let us be the first to connect to the new Western and Atlantic Railway, now known as the state road. Let us decide our future tonight. Vote yes for the extension to Terminus."

The connection to the state road was Thomson's brain-child. It was the essence of Edgar Thomson. Throughout his life, his brilliance and legendary vision were obvious to the dullest of minds. Thomson paused and quickly thought to himself, *"No one else in the company had followed the state's plans. No one else had given this brilliant opportunity any thought.*

"When our charter was first amended in 1836, I had my preamble added to it. I was the only one who desired to connect with the state road at Terminus. We have reached the time to decide where we shall place our road beyond Madison. I know where I would locate it. This decision will determine the future of our company.

"The stockholders are aware that the people of the West have proposed to have a series of railroads made to connect Cincinnati to the southern Atlantic Coast. Those people believe that the best route for this road would be through the state of Georgia. It is imperative that our road be a part of that road. They are correct, this is the best route. I am positive that our railroad must be a link in that connection, or we are out of business. We would be a vital link. What a money-maker! Cincinnati, Ohio, straight through to Savannah, Georgia. Unbelievable!

"Look at a map, gentlemen, and see if I am not correct. These stockholders had better approve this extension, or we will have to turn our leaders out, or I may be out myself."

Thomson posed the question to the stockholders. "I call upon you to carry the vote to join the state road. We are only sixty-five miles from completing the connection and the remaining cost will not exceed $1,200,000. That is an amount so trifling, compared with the immense benefits which will result to you stockholders that I cannot believe there will be any difficulty obtaining it."

The vote to extend the line was approved by the stockholders. The Georgia state legislature had already approved another act giving the company the right to continue westward from Madison, to pass through or near Covington, and to connect with and join the railroad being built by the State. All the stockholders of the Georgia Railroad had to do was approve it.

Construction contracts were let from Greensboro to Madison, another twenty miles down the line. A stroke of good luck for the company occurred; the planters near the Athens branch were hiring their slaves out to do the grading there. The selling price of cotton was so low at the time that it was more profitable to hire them out than to plant cotton.

More than eighty-seven miles of track were in operation by the end of 1838. There was no way to separate the income and expenses of the railroad and the banking operations at that time, but their combined profit was $112,000 for 1838.

Thomson received a raise to $5,000 per year in January of 1839. No one made more in the transportation business. However, due to the worsening economic conditions impacting the company, a newly-established retrenchment committee reported in July of 1839, that salary reductions were a necessity.

On September the 10th, the Board told Thomson, "Sir, your salary is twice that of the president of the company, and we have no recourse other than to put you on notice that you must begin paying your own expenses. At this time we shall not approve any further westward expansion. We do not have the funds and we don't know when or where we'll get them."

In October, the Board threw out the retrenchment plan, decided to cut all salaries twenty percent, then changed their minds and said the stockholders needed to make those decisions. It was evident that they were reacting, indeed surrendering, to the financial crisis of the Panic of 1837 and its ongoing after-effects. The crushing despondency it created throughout the country would be felt through the end of 1841.

The Board soon made an unexpected announcement. "Mr. Thomson, we have now decided to approve the request you've been pushing to survey the line west from Madison to meet the Western and Atlantic at Terminus. Additionally, you are now authorized to let the construction contracts for the superstructure between Greensboro and Madison. Our sincere best wishes are extended to you and we acknowledge the superb job you have done, and are doing, for the company. We are here to support you."

To further illustrate their complete confusion over their monetary problems, the Board then declared a four percent dividend.

The remaining fourteen miles of road was completed to Greensboro in 1839, and the company received its first contract to haul the United States Mail. A night train from Augusta to Greensboro was begun to handle the new business. At Greensboro the mail was disbursed throughout the state via stagecoach lines. In 1839, a three and one half mile branch from Camak to Warrenton was also opened.

The Eatonton branch, which was to be built per the state charter, was put on hold so that the company could concentrate on completing the Madison line to Terminus on the Chattahoochee. By the time the Georgia Railroad decided to proceed with the Eatonton branch, the city already had a railroad connecting it to Milledgeville. The Georgia Railroad branch to Eatonton was never built.

To complicate the completion of the final sixty-five miles to Terminus, many of the men contracted yellow fever in the field. No one had a clue what this yellow fever was, but the men were sick and their work suffered. They were not alone. On June 8, 1839, members of an Augusta family living by the river on Lincoln Street were attacked by a disease thought to be a "remittent fever."

On July 5, 1839, laborers working in the same vicinity were also attacked. A little boy playing in the same area was the next victim. He was taken to a doctor with the same symptoms as the other victims and died in a few days. His delicate little skin turned a bright yellow toward the end of his illness. He developed large purple blotches shortly after his death like many cases occurring in that part of the city.

On August the 19th, Augusta's mayor called together all the physicians of the city and said, "Gentlemen, we have had forty cases of this disease in the city to date and it is spreading rapidly. I believe I can, and, therefore, I am, at this very moment, declaring this an epidemic. I need your help. The whole city needs your help. I am asking Dr. Joseph Eve to head up a committee of three doctors to investigate this disease and to provide direction to us. Dr. Eve has some of the best doctors and professors in the country working with him at the Medical College. With their expertise, I'm sure the cause and the cure will soon be found."

The committee was, of course, diligent in its pursuit of the origins and the makeup of this mysterious disease called "the black vomit." Dr. Milton Antony, the founder of the Medical College of Georgia ten years earlier, read from his notes to the other committee doctors. "From 1768 through 1838, there have been twenty-seven yellow fever outbreaks in

Charleston, only 136 miles from Augusta. Yet, there were no outbreaks in Augusta during that period. In 1833, the railway connecting Charleston to Hamburg was opened and is now in full operation. Today the distance can be covered in just a few hours.

"What does this mean? There have been no restrictions whatsoever on railroad travel to Hamburg. This year the fever has raged in Charleston, and Augusta has had its first outbreak. The facts seem to bear out that the transmission of the fever is caused by something connected to the railroad and its speed. Transmission of the disease by personal contact is not shown to exist. Too many Charlestonians have fled to Augusta and then died. But no Augustans in contact with them have died. What are we up against?

"Here are some troubling facts. The transportation agent in Thomson who opened and unloaded the freight cars from Augusta was recently stricken with a fever. He and his wife, whose job it was to enter the rail cars and serve refreshments to the passengers, have both died of yellow fever. Along the opened parts of the Georgia Railroad, all railroad employees who slept near the depots in the freight cars arriving from Augusta were attacked with the fever; those who slept elsewhere were not attacked. A young farmer in Camak slept in a passenger car overnight and died eight days later of yellow fever. What is the connection?"

The two other doctors read from their findings which were all similar to Dr. Antony's in content. They had interviewed many Augustans and were unanimous in their conclusions. Dr. Eve submitted their report to the mayor on August 29, 1839.

"Mr. Mayor, our committee has completed the report you requested of us concerning the outbreak of yellow fever in the city. It is twenty-eight pages in length and contains much detail. Let me now just give you our findings in brief and allow you the opportunity to study the report at your convenience. We will each be available to answer any questions in the following days that you or our civic leaders may have.

"We find that this epidemic has not been introduced into the city by any foreign sources, meaning human contact, in particular. We, therefore, state that this disease is not contagious. It is not spread by breath or touch.

"We are also confident in reporting that the cause of this epidemic originates from the foul and deadly vapors emerging from the accumulation of the city's trash piled up between Lincoln and Elbert Streets. The 200,000 cubic feet of spoiled vegetable and animal matter at the upper trash wharf is producing the vile atmosphere using sunlight as a catalyst. This deadly trash has been collected from the city's lots, both occupied and vacant, since 1834.

"Nothing has been done to date by the city to remove that cancerous refuse from our midst. We recommend that you push to build a city pier near the trash pile and have all the trash thrown into the river. The sooner this is done, the sooner we feel that the city will be safe again. We cannot estimate how many more cases we'll see this year, or how many people will die. We do not know how long this epidemic will last, but removing that trash will be the first step in ending it."

A cold, killing frost ended the epidemic in Augusta on November 8, 1839. Between 1,500 and 2,000 cases of yellow fever were reported. Deaths from the fever reached 240 before it was over. It revisited Augusta and its surrounding areas year after year. The trash pile clean-up improved the quality of the air and the general appearance of Augusta. It was not the cure for yellow fever, unfortunately.

Dr. Milton Antony died September 19, 1839, less than one month after his committee's report was submitted to the mayor. He had been sick for seven days. His skin was bright yellow, like fresh butter, with little button-like purple spots all over him. The cause of death was yellow fever.

9 Insider Dealings, Railroad Barons, Augusta Take-Over, and Gold

In 1840, Edgar Thomson appointed a twenty-three-year old, hard-working, self-made son of Maine as the assistant engineer of the Georgia Railroad. In just one year he had worked himself up from rodman on the Philadelphia and Reading Railroad to the position of assistant engineer, through study and hard work. Lemuel P. Grant became one of Thomson's fast friends and a fellow investor.

Thomson had so much confidence in Grant's ability that his designated section of the road's engineers was given the task of locating the line between Madison and Atlanta in 1840. When that was accomplished, Grant moved briefly to the Central Railroad as an assistant engineer, but he returned to the Georgia in 1843. He left for more money, but Thomson brought him back with the lure of even more money.

Grant oversaw the grading of the road until it was finished at Marthasville. Thomson was deeply pleased with Grant's work, but his personal affinity for him came about through their mutual speculation in land in the path of the road and near it. Thomson had always purchased land in the direction in which the road was heading and he found a kindred spirit in Grant.

"I'm telling you, Thomson." Grant said, "We will make a fortune on this one. I'm buying a couple of large parcels in Marthasville, and I'll handle the same deal for you if you want me to. I'm buying lots 44, 52 and 53 totaling six hundred acres. You won't believe what they cost. One tract is only seventy-five cents an acre, and the other two are two dollars an acre.

"I think they're so lovely that I may eventually build a nice house there and settle down. Who knows; it's so pretty there, one day I may build a park, too. Or maybe I'll give a hundred acres or so to the city, assuming there will be a city eventually, and let them build the park. They could name it after me. Marthasville's Grant Park; how's that sound? Are you in?"

Thomson shook his head and said, "Yes, see if you can get me several hundred acres, too, at near the same price."

Grant was obviously pleased that Thomson wanted in and replied, "Fine, I'll make arrangements for five or six hundred acres in your name. You won't regret it."

Thomson's private business and his professional duties to the railroad always overlapped. It was hard to see where one transaction began and another ended. He was constantly buying land in the path of its future development. He knew where the road was being located, but the general public didn't. Thomson and a few of his hand-picked business friends kept the future location of the line top secret. They didn't want their competitors to know where the road was going.

For the sake of convenience, Thomson at times did buy land in his name which was legitimately for the railroad. Later, when time permitted, he would transfer it to the company. Thomson was becoming well-known in the country's financial centers. He owed that to his growing wealth and his exploitation of insider investment opportunities. Thomson certainly profited from his position as chief engineer of the railroad, and he took advantage of all the opportunities his position afforded him. In spite of that, he always tried to maintain an ethical line between his private and public responsibilities. In that respect, Edgar Thomson was a virtual saint compared to the self-dealings of his contemporaries.

Thomson bought a considerable amount of common stock in the

Georgia Railroad and Banking Company. He also bought a lot of stock in other companies, but he usually invested or speculated in only railroad stock. He would invest a sizable sum in a railroad he had targeted, get on its Board of Directors and then use his influence to get a crony appointed to an inside position. The weight of his reputation was all that was needed to get employees hired at other companies.

Once his crony was established, he would feed Thomson inside information as to the results of operations. He would also inform Thomson of his opinion as to whether Thomson should sell or trade his stock, or whether Thomson should increase his shares to affect a takeover of the company. Thomson's takeover of a company did not mean he would get the Georgia Railroad to gain control of the targeted company. No, these would be personal deals wherein Edgar Thomson would become the President, if he thought it expedient, of the targeted company. There would be no transactions in which the Georgia Railroad was a party.

Why would Thomson do that? By having an inside connection, Thomson was given the advantage of not having to venture a great amount of money into a company until he knew it was a winner. He did on many occasions take a loss on these manipulations, but seldom a large one.

Thomson would have complete control as to expansions of these other lines. He would have them make business decisions that would put them in a position where they could expand their road so that in the future, only known to Thomson, they would join the Georgia Railroad as a connecting road. Yes, these companies all had legitimate Boards of Directors, but Thomson's influence was so great that he could make anything he wished occur. He was not out to make these companies fail; he was out to make them profitable and to tie in with his line. Then all the companies would be profitable. Connecting to the Georgia would help the targeted company by increasing its traffic and revenues. It would help the Georgia by the same token. It would also make both companies' stocks in Thomson's portfolio double, triple, or quadruple in value.

In later years, Thomson turned down an offer to invest in land on which he would have to locate a depot to make a profit. He wrote his friend, "It would not be right for me to enter into the speculation. I must not only be pure in these matters but seem so, also."

Thomson invested heavily in private companies that developed new technology which might eventually become useful to railways. Technology that might be useful to any railway, not just Thomson's company, or its suppliers or lessees. He would not speculate in his own railroad company's stocks or bonds. He would never sell his company's stock short like his many later colleagues would do.

Cornelius Vanderbilt, Jay Gould, and Leland Stanford, to name a few, all became enormously wealthy by dealing in the stock of their own companies. Andrew Carnegie, one of Thomson's best friends, asked Thomson to trade some railroad bonds in one of his investments for another's, a move which would have helped Carnegie.

Thomson wrote Carnegie and declined. He shared with his friend a piece of personal philosophy; if Thomson had taken a different path in his business dealings, like his contemporaries, he would be sitting at home now counting his tens of millions of dollars.

Those men, plus Mark Hopkins, C. P. Huntington, Charles Crocker, and Cyrus Holliday, all shared an ability to spread new railroads all over the land. To enable them to do this, they bought Congressmen and hounded Presidents. They ruined trusted associates as quick as a wink. They built the nation's railroads; more squeamish men would have failed. Those early railroad barons had made their first small fortunes as merchants and traders. They parlayed these first fortunes into wealth untold, unlike many men who had squandered theirs in stupid future investments. They saw themselves as historical figures who would unite distant people and put an end to tribalism and hatred.

In their own eyes, these railroad barons were not wicked men. The desire to fulfill the nation's destiny of a railroad system to the Pacific coast made the best of these men greedy and cruel. Their destiny just didn't coincide with the destiny of the poor. Their code was the simple law of the rich get richer. To them the pursuit of wealth by a few entrepreneurs was the major process by which a civilization perfected itself.

This view of life, called Social Darwinism, made avarice a virtue. Social Darwinism taunted traditional business ethics as a silly game to be played in the quest for life's riches. It advocated that fierce, constant competition was the only way to achieve great wealth, life's greatest reward.

Edgar Thomson was never like those men. He was not a greedy, self-obsessed ogre who would do anything to increase his wealth. He was, however, absolutely cost conscious in building and maintaining his railroad, just as the other barons were, and that included paying as few wages as was possible to obtain labor. The railroad empires were built by the backs of the ignorant immigrants who, unfortunately, had no other means to provide for themselves and their families. The immigrants were joined in the North by city slum dwellers, and in the South by bonded African slaves.

The great charitable and philanthropic works these mighty railroad barons performed after they had accumulated their individual wealth paled in comparison with the heartache and pitiful lives their laborers bore to make it. It was, and still is, easy to praise the works of individual and corporate charity without knowing how the funds necessary to complete those works was raised.

Those line workers on the road suffered many calamities as the road was built. Thomson sent the directors an operating report describing the on-going, but nearly ended, deadly yellow fever situation in the field. "Mr. Camak, please send my regards to the Board. I have not had an opportunity to return to Augusta these last two weeks due to the burden of pushing our last sixty-five miles forward. If you please, tell the Board that even though our men were working a hundred miles from Augusta, many of the track-layers still became sick with this yellow fever, or black vomit, as they call it down here.

"Fortunately, by nursing and resting our sick men in the few houses and tavern rooms around, we have had only two deaths. They were both

Irish gandy dancers. The Negro slave laborers seem to be immune to it; they look upon it as a curiosity and call it yellow jack. The dead will be returned to Augusta for burial tomorrow morning with our next shipment of construction reports and accounting invoices. We shall be at one hundred percent in the morning."

In 1841, great progress was made, and trains were running on the completed road to Athens. The track was laid and ready to open from Greensboro to Madison. Unfortunately for Thomson's timetable and pocketbook, a problem with the location caused a delay in laying the track farther up the road.

"Gentlemen, in our final sixty-five miles of the road to Terminus, thirteen of them have had to pass through the valley of the Alcovy and Yellow Rivers. The land here has required larger bridges and more rock cuts than I anticipated. This has made construction more time-consuming and more expensive. The delay on this stretch is unfortunate, but it will not be unreasonably long in endurance. I look forward to seeing each of you when a break appears."

During the great depression the country was enduring, things had gotten financially worse for many of the company's stockholders, most of whom were afraid for the company and themselves. A difference of opinion on company policy and expansion had created a rift between the Athens stockholders and the Augusta stockholders.

"We Augustans, backed by most of the stockholders from Savannah, want no further expansion of our road at present. We want it to stop, and now. You Athenians have not suffered as hard economically as the rest of us in the other parts of Georgia. We all know your economy is more diverse, and is not dependent primarily on cotton, like ours. You know, as well as we do, that the price of cotton has fallen through the floor. We are in perilous times. We do not want the company to take on any more debt or risks, at this time. We want the road to stop now. At least until things get better."

The Athenians wanted to continue the company's expansion to the state road. This fight between the Augustans and the Athenians was not the only fight on the horizon.

At the meeting when the Board approved Thomson's expansion to Terminus in 1841, they told him to implement an austerity measure and to save as much money as he could. That resolution came while Thomson was diligently working as hard as he ever had, and it led to bitter words between Thomson and the directors. Thomson, throughout his life, could never accept anyone doubting him or his ability.

The directors then voted not to pay the scheduled October, 1841, dividends to the stockholders. When the stockholders were informed, they were livid. To them that was the straw that finally broke the camel's back. "I'll tell you the truth, sir. As a stockholder, I am sick of the obvious inability of these directors to provide direction for our company. I am also sick over the non-payment of my dividend. I need that money to pay some bills that have been piling up. Am I going to have to sell my shares to do it?"

The Augustans were often seen huddled up and grumbling together. "We have used our money to purchase more company stock over the years than those Athenians. We have bought control of the company. What was the sense of us buying our stock if we don't have any say at all in running it? Let's take control and make some of the changes that we want. Let's install a new Board of Directors during this year's meeting. We do not need to wait any longer. Here's what we need. One, Edgar Thomson has got to go. Two, we need to replace James Camak with Judge King as president. And, three, we need to move the company's banking headquarters from Athens to Augusta. Camak and his Athens cronies are going to ruin us."

At the company's beginning, only one director was from Augusta; all the others were from the area surrounding Athens. Nothing was going on, so that was fine. Once the road was started, everything occurred around Augusta. Besides, the Athens branch was not even started and Augustans now controlled the stock.

Although the Athenians lost their control of the Board in 1840, the Board continued to meet in Athens until May of 1841. Only Athenians attended the meetings; even Thomson appeared at only three in all of 1840. The company's principal bank was in Athens with a branch in Augusta. In October of 1843, the directors decided to move the annual meeting to Augusta.

At the December, 1841, yearly meeting, the company's stockholders voted to retain Edgar Thomson's professional services as Chief Engineer, but they reduced his salary to $3,000 per year. They elected a new Board of Directors, and Thomson lost his seat. Augusta Judge John Pendleton King was elected company president.

The $2,000 salary reduction made Thomson aware that the stockholders had considered doing away with him. Thomson was outraged. He slowly simmered until the first meeting of the new directors on May 12th, 1842, and then he submitted his resignation, effective immediately. The Board was caught off guard, undecided whether to accept it.

It was finally decided to have three Board members meet with Thomson and see if they could talk him into staying. They had some success; he agreed to stay if he could take several months off to go up North on private business. Upon his return, he signed a contract to remain as Chief Engineer at a salary of $3,000 per year until the road was completed.

Thomson was anxious to head back to his boyhood home. The small farm on the Baltimore Post Road about ten miles from Philadelphia had been in the Thomson family ever since the first Thomson had come over with William Penn. It was here that Edgar Thomson had been born on February 10, 1808.

Now, at thirty-four, Thomson had been almost constantly away from home for fifteen years. The home place was in the heavily Quaker region of the Delaware Valley, and the thought of its pastoral setting was deeply ingrained in Thomson's consciousness. The farm was sold in 1842, and much to his own amazement, the normally unsentimental Thomson rushed home and bought it back. It remained in his hands until his death in 1874. He hired an overseer to raise a few cows and horses on the farm to make it look like it was a real enterprise.

The mystery was why the farm had to be sold in the first place. Were there no communications between Thomson and his family? Why hadn't he been informed of the pending sale? Maybe he had, and wasn't interested and had just ignored it. Or maybe he had a change of heart at the last minute which required his immediate departure to Pennsylvania to repurchase it. Certainly he couldn't have been that busy.

Edgar Thomson and his colleagues were constantly buying and selling investments during the entire time they were surveying and constructing the railroad. Chief railroad engineers and their cronies all over the country bought for their own portfolios the lands that lay in the path of their roads' routes. Almost always they bought before the locations were made public. This was using insider information for personal gain.

"I do not think that there is anything inappropriate in a railroad engineer's buying public land for his own benefit. Some people have said that it is not right for an employee of a railroad to make a profit buying land in the undisclosed location of the route of the road. I say that it has been done since the beginning of the canal and railroad systems everywhere. It has never been seen as a dishonest thing to do," Thomson told James Camak when questioned about the industrywide practice.

Thomson bought tremendous acres of timberland, not just in the path of the road, but also all around its future location. It was to be used in constructing the ties and the buildings along the road. Thomson's timber was cut to the railroad's specifications right there beside the road during construction and sold to the railroad. As the road moved west, new Thomson timberland was used.

"I charge my company only the going rate for my timber sold to them. The going rate is computed by the timber costs and the freight charged to get a timely delivery to the site. By having the local timber from my land purchased by my railroad, I can maximize my profits. The normal shipping costs, let's say from Augusta to Berzelia, are included in the price, but in reality there are no shipping costs. Everybody in the industry does it."

By 1842, Thomson had come to know as many men as anyone in the eastern part of middle Georgia. One of the influential businessmen with whom he had been dickering over an investment possibility was Jeremiah Griffin. Thomson had been trying since 1839 to convince Griffin that they should work together to issue stock in a gold mining company and to begin mining immediately.

Mr. Griffin had purchased three thousand acres of supposedly gold-enriched lands in northern Columbia County bordering the Little River. It sounded like a good deal for Mr. Griffin, but it shut out all other prospectors who might have mined the whole area. Therefore, it prevented a gold rush which would have been a boon to the entire region.

Griffin explained it all to Thomson when they first met. "Here's the deal, Mr. Thomson. I bought all this land back in 1826. These two English men came through here peddling pots and pans and ran up on some quartz covered in gold. That was about three years before. We called that 'the 40 acre lot.'

"Those boys didn't have no money and couldn't buy the land. There wasn't no state lottery yet, so they couldn't stake a claim and start digging. They tried to talk the farmers into selling them the land on shares, but the farmers didn't care nothing about gold mining. Them English fellows took off to strike it rich out West. Well, I've done pretty well by farming, and I could afford the whole kit and caboodle, so I bought three thousand acres and dug this mine.

"I became a gold miner, but I was still a farmer. Me and some of the boys piddled around for a while, but we never did get into the swing of things. I bought those boys out in 1833, and it's just been me ever since. I quit that placer-mining that they was doing and built me a stamp mill.

"With that stamp mill, which was the first one ever built in these United States, I cleared over $80,000 profit. Now you come here asking me to let you and your friends buy in and sell shares to the public. I ask you, Mr. Thomson, just how much money do I need? Where would I spend it and on what?"

Thomson had given up on incorporating Griffin's gold-mining lands. Griffin had greatly enlarged his operations and was very successful. In 1842, while returning home to Georgia after looking at the actual day-to-day operation of a very innovative piece of gold-mining equipment, Griffin met with disaster.

He had been riding alone on horseback for two days and was halfway home from Alabama. In the early morning, with the new day's sun just clearing the horizon, Griffin gave his horse its lead and it walked right up on a ten-foot diamondback rattler. The horse jumped at the sound of the snake's rattles. Griffin reached for his pistol in its saddle holster. The noise was deafening as the pistol went off. It had not cleared his holster. The ball entered Griffin's right thigh halfway between his knee and his crotch, hitting a major artery. As the blood poured from his body, Griffin slumped off his horse and onto the ground. The situation was hopeless. He bled out and died right on that spot.

Thomson was sorry to hear that Mr. Griffin had died, but he hoped there was a chance that Griffin's wife would sell the gold-bearing land to him. He had to try. By the time Thomson and one of his assistant engineers got to the family home site near the mine, Mr. Griffin's will had been read. His entire fortune, which included his mines, was left entirely to his numerous heirs.

Those industrious people had already selected which of the six mines they wanted. They told Thomson that they were sorry he had come all that way for nothing, but there was no way anyone outside the family was going to mine near them. The land was not for sale, under any circumstances.

10 Dahlonega Gold and The Trail Of Tears

In June of 1842, Samuel Mitchell and Charles Garner wanted to honor Wilson Lumpkin, a respected civic leader in the state and a key man in the development of Georgia's state railroad, the Western and Atlantic. Samuel Mitchell had donated a large tract of land to the state for the road, and Charles Garner was the railroad's Chief Engineer. Lumpkin was best known to Mitchell and Garner as the general manager of the Western and Atlantic Railroad of the State of Georgia and the key advocate in improving transportation in the state.

The two men decided to honor Mr. Lumpkin by renaming Terminus, changing it to Marthasville, after his youngest daughter, Martha. People began calling the tiny settlement Marthasville immediately, but it wasn't legally incorporated until December of 1843. Its name would be changed to Atlanta in December, 1847, thanks to Edgar Thomson.

Wilson Lumpkin was a very prominent political leader in antebellum Georgia. He had been a state senator four times, a Georgia governor two times, a trustee of the University of Georgia, and the U. S. Commissioner to the Cherokees from 1836—1837. Lumpkin was a U. S. senator from 1837—1841, and afterwards, was the surveyor of record in determining Georgia's sovereign borders.

Growing up in Virginia, and in Wilkes and Oglethorpe Counties in

Georgia, Lumpkin saw many deadly acts committed by Indians against their neighboring whites. He said he could never forget those acts. He came to believe that the white and red populations of America could never live together in peace. Because of this belief, Lumpkin played a major role in the final removal of the Cherokees in north Georgia in 1838 and 1839. This infamous act was called the Trail of Tears. Lumpkin did not hate the Indians; he actually considered himself a humanitarian.

He may have considered also that the Dahlonega gold rush occurred right in the middle of tens of thousands of acres of Cherokee land. That was land, all state politicians and businessmen thought, that needed to be opened to white goldminers and settlers. Humanitarian or not, Lumpkin was swayed by the political pressure placed upon him to open that extremely valuable Indian land.

The Georgia gold rush started in 1829 when a Milledgeville newspaper printed a bulletin reporting two gold mines had been discovered in Habersham County. The paper said what everyone originally had thought had come to pass: the gold region of North and South Carolina was found to reach into Georgia.

By late 1829, thousands of prospectors had rushed into the Cherokee Nation lusting for gold. By 1830, there were four thousand miners working along the Yahoola Creek alone. Any sane person could see that there was no possibility that the Indians could remain in their native land.

Gold rush towns sprang up quickly, especially near the rush's center in Lumpkin County. Auraria became an instant boomtown, growing to 1,000 persons by 1832. In 1833, Licklog, the county seat, was renamed Dahlonega for the Cherokee word meaning golden. Within a few months, 1,000 people lived there and about 5,000 lived in the surrounding counties.

The Dahlonega Mint was established by the Federal government in 1838. It coined more than $100,000 in gold in its first year. By the early 1840s, the Dahlonega gold rush had played out. The miners tore out for California as soon as word of the great 1849 gold strikes reached town.

They had made Georgia the leading gold-producing state until the 1849 California rush.

John C. Calhoun purchased a North Georgia gold mine and made a fortune. As one of his many assets, it was part of the estate he left his daughter, Anna Maria. Anna married a Philadelphia-born, European-educated engineer named Thomas Green Clemson.

Living on the family plantation in South Carolina, Clemson became a longtime advocate for an agricultural college in the Upstate of Carolina. In 1889, Thomas Green Clemson left his entire estate to found the Clemson Agricultural College of South Carolina. His estate had been endowed by assets of his father-in-law, his wife, and his own.

Wilson Lumpkin said repeatedly that by moving the Cherokees out west they could develop a culture of their own that would be equal to the white man's. However, he had made a big mistake; the Cherokees already had a culture of their own that was equal to the white man's.

In the 1790s, the Federal government sent agents into the Cherokee nation to teach them proper farming techniques and trade skills. Beginning in the 1820s, the Cherokees operated their own mills, businesses, farms, and plantations. They had access to missionary schools and churches in their own communities. They had their own language and their own constitution.

Lumpkin said a new state out west populated only by Indians could eventually become a state on par with all the others in the country. Native Americans were forced at gunpoint out of their homeland in the southern part of the Great Appalachian Valley. It was inevitable; it could not be stopped. The white settlers of America wanted to have all land east of the Mississippi River opened for white expansion.

The primary push was to remove the Cherokees from northern Georgia, eastern Tennessee, and western North Carolina. Andrew Jackson was elected President running on the platform of removing all Indians from their ancestral lands. Jackson's support primarily came from those easterners and southerners who wanted the Indians moved beyond the Mississippi River. The push began in the early 1830s, and soon some smaller Indian tribes accepted money and western land for their agreement to sell their homeland to the U. S. government. Speaking as a white politician and businessman, John C. Calhoun argued that "our mission is to occupy this vast continental domain."

Among those southerners who campaigned for the removal of the Native Americans were the Georgians engaged to build the railroad from Augusta to Marthasville. When the line was completed, and connected with the new railroad from Chattanooga to Marthasville, Augusta would have a continuous rail line from Augusta all the way to Chattanooga. It was only natural that those businessmen had a vested interest in seeing that the proposed connecting state railroad through north Georgia would have its route free of Indians. A passenger on the railroad from Augusta couldn't get to Cincinnati or Pittsburgh if it only ran to Marthasville and then stopped. That's what would happen if another railroad couldn't go north because of hostile Indians attacking the train. Thomson and all the other railroad executives wanted lucrative, profitable long-term routes, not little fifty or hundred mile roads which barely broke even.

Edgar Thomson actively petitioned President Jackson to remove the Indians. Jackson, as we all know, was from Tennessee and was, therefore, very interested in having the Nashville (Tennessee) and Chattanooga (Tennessee) Railway completed. It was strictly business. Could he have been heavily invested in the N & C? Yes. Could he have received substantial gifts to see it a certain way? Yes.

The N & C's stock records wouldn't necessarily have shown his name if he were a stockholder. Many times investors put stock in the names of their cronies to keep their competitors from knowing what they were up to. Edgar Thomson did just that over and over again.

The Southern political leaders, the business leaders of the North and the South, and white settlers worked together to pressure Jackson. All they cared about was the almighty dollar; there were many fortunes to be made from the buying and selling of the lands vacated by the Indians.

In the 1820s, Andrew Jackson and a business partner overtly bought and sold much land reserved for the Choctaws and Chickasaws in western Tennessee. He, therefore, had no trouble as President signing the "Indian Removal Act" in 1830. Martin Van Buren, Jackson's Vice President in 1832, continued the Indian policies as Jackson had insisted when he gave Van Buren his considerable support. In 1838, Van Buren completed Jackson's Indian policy by actually signing the legislation requiring that the Cherokees begin their journey on the Trail of Tears.

It was a great plan for almost everyone—everyone white, that is. The plan was to buy up the Indian lands, to build railroads so the new settlers could get to those lands, and to push the European hordes westward to buy that same land from the speculators. The only problem was how the politicians could physically get the Indians off their land.

The Cherokees of Georgia, having a culture that matched the white man's, used the white man's methods to resist. They showed they were no frontier savages. They had developed their own written language, they printed their own newspaper, and they elected tribal leaders to their own representative government. When the government of Georgia refused to recognize them as a sovereign state and threatened to take their land by force, the Cherokees took their grievances to the U. S. Supreme Court where they won.

John Marshall, in his opinion in *Cherokee Nation v. Georgia*, stated that Georgia had no jurisdiction over the Cherokees and had no claims to their lands. The white people of Georgia and their politicians ignored the decision. Good ole Andy Jackson didn't lift a finger to enforce one bit of it. Jackson was livid at the Marshall court's agreement with the Cherokees' position and supposedly said publicly, "Marshall had made his decision; now let him enforce it!"

In 1831, forced removal of the Choctaws from their land by the U. S. Army began. They were marched to Oklahoma. By 1832, the Cherokee land lottery had distributed all Cherokee lands to white Georgians. During the Trail of Tears in 1838 and 1839, some 20,000 Cherokees were rounded up like wild horses. At gunpoint they too were herded to Oklahoma. Nearly 5,000 died on the forced march, from the elements, from fatigue, or from disease.

The survivors were led to a completely foreign land where they were supposed to once again become farmers and ranchers like the white men who had virtually robbed them. It was an impossible task at that time at their new location. In the heat and in the cold of their new barren homeland, they ate rotten horseflesh to survive.

While some Indian tribes did not fight to stay on their lands, many of the Seminoles of Florida under Chief Osceola did. They waged all-out war well into the 1840s against white soldiers. William T. Sherman said, "The more we can kill this year, the less will have to be killed in the next war. They all have to be killed or be maintained as a species of paupers." Nearly three thousand Seminoles left their ancestral land and headed west. But approximately five hundred Seminoles never surrendered and moved to the Everglades to continue their fight which finally ended in their defeat in 1842.

11 Spanish Cruelty, The Five Civilized Tribes, and Indian Practices

This chapter is taken from various sources, including a first hand memoir of a trader in the mid to late 1700's. I include it here to give some background that many are unaware of about the relationships of the earlier settlers with the Indians. It also gives some background of the Spaniards' role in early fighting with the Indians. If this is not of interest to you, skip this chapter and move on to Chapter Twelve.

*Throughout the Augusta to Terminus area, there had been many con-*frontations between the whites and the Indians. A few renegade groups of Indians still harassed white people, but usually only for trinkets they could steal and resell. Edgar Thomson always remembered an event he had witnessed when he had just arrived at Augusta. He was in a tavern downtown with a couple of new acquaintances and one of the bargemen from the river had come in with his cronies. These rough men loaded and unloaded the keel-boats and towed them when the river ran too strong for the steamboats and paddle-wheelers. The men were coarse and ferocious; their chief occupation seemed to consist of drinking, fighting, and gambling.

One man, who was half drunk, was bragging about recently killing an innocent Indian. He said he hid in some woods skirting the road to

Macon and shot the Indian as he passed by. The Indian had not suspected any trouble as he returned to his home from hunting; this was a time of peace. He carried a huge wild turkey over his shoulder. The waterman said he threw the Indian's body into a thicket and took the bird home for his supper. He was proud of his accomplishment and said he would just as soon kill an Indian as a fox or an otter. Thomson thought the man was making a jest, but Thomson's acquaintances told him it was true. The man had neither been tried nor punished. The murderer in that day was called a Christian, and his victim a heathen.

In his *Memoirs, or my Sojourn in the Creek Nation* written by Louis LeClerc Milfort, the story of the demise of the Southeastern Native Americans was given from an eye-witness account and perspective. The French lost Canada in the French and Indian War and gave up all hope of developing Louisiana and the South as their future domain. Without French help, which had been substantial, the Indians could not stop the Spanish from controlling Florida.

The priests that accompanied the Spanish soldiers undertook to convert the Indians to Christianity. They began with a mild but persuasive teaching to the women in order to win their confidence. Then they baptized them and required them to go to confession. They introduced them to many rituals which their simple manner could not comprehend. The priests taught the women that many of their past traditions were criminal. The priests taught the women not to comply with their husbands' wishes.

The husbands understood from whence the new hostility in their marriages came, and banned all priests from entering their homes. The priests resorted to an inquisition, an American Inquisition, and many disobedient Indians were burned at the stake. The Indians rose up in fury with spears and arrows, but were beaten down by Spanish swords and muskets.

Having no place to turn except death, these Florida Indians called on their enemy, the Creeks, to help them. The Creeks, who had no love for the Spanish, sent some warriors to attack the Spanish. Despite having superior forces, the Spanish were defeated and ran off, leaving their forts and cannons, but not until they mined their forts with explosives.

As the unaware Creeks entered the fort, the explosives went off, killing many of the warriors. Angered and outraged by this terrorism and wanting to avenge their dead brothers, the Indians fell upon the unfortunate Spanish inhabitants of the forts and massacred everyone as they fled. The victory over the Spanish ruined Spanish trade in the New World, which opened a stable environment between the Indians and the English.

These Apalachee and Florida Indians were jointly called Seminoles, or strangers, by the Creeks. In gratitude for the Creeks' help against the Spanish, the Seminoles asked to unite with the Creeks as one nation. The Creek elders in council agreed, but said that the Seminoles should keep their own name.

The Creek Nation, augmented by a tremendous number of immigrants like the Seminoles from neighboring nations, became the most powerful nation of Native Americans. They were the largest of the Five Civilized Tribes which were the Chickasaws, the Choctaws, the Muskogees, the Cherokees and the Creeks. The Chickasaws lived in present-day Arkansas; the Choctaws in present-day Louisiana and Alabama; the Muskogees also in present-day Alabama; the Cherokees in present-day North Carolina, Tennessee, and northern Georgia; and the Creeks everywhere else in present-day Alabama and Georgia.

Early historians split the Indian culture into two distinct groups. They were either referred to as "wild" or as "civilized." What made white people think Indians were wild or savages, or what made them think they were civilized? How could they judge? These white people weren't all that civilized themselves at that time. Wasn't it like the pot calling the kettle black?

They were called the Five Civilized Tribes because they had adopted many of the white man's ways of living. Most of the civilized tribesmen had converted to Christianity, they were literate, they intermarried with white Americans, and they practiced plantation slavery practices. The civilized tribes had written constitutions and had centralized governments. They engaged in business with the whites to both peoples' benefits. As their greatest attribute, in the opinion of most white Americans, they maintained stable economic and political relations with England.

Who first tried to civilize the Indians? Our greatest American, George Washington, said that the American Indians were the white man's equal. He formulated and implemented a plan to civilize them. Thomas Jefferson continued Washington's plan when he took the Presidency. Both men thought that once the Indians embraced the concept of privately-owned property, built houses, began farming, educated their children, and became Christians that they would be totally accepted by white America.

That would probably have worked had it not been for the hordes of so-called civilized white men who greedily and illegally invaded their lands. In their quest for the riches of gold and their hopes of fortunes made from land expansion and speculation, the white men pushed beyond the legitimate frontiers set by governmental treaties made in good faith with the Indians.

Milfort in his *Memoirs* tells how he and ten savages were taking official dispatches to some commissioners trying to find peace between the Creeks and the Americans. When they arrived, one savage spied a beautiful horse a white soldier was riding and demanded it be returned to him. He said it was his and had been stolen. Milfort knew him and believed him.

The dispute was turned over to the commissioners. The Indian said he had raised the horse from birth and still had its mother. To convince the commissioners, he requested to be permitted to bring in fifty witnesses to prove his case. Before that could be accomplished, the white man left and returned with twenty white men who said their comrade had raised the horse. The whites all swore on a Bible that they were telling the truth. Milfort told the Indian what had happened and that he would have to give up the horse.

The Indian pondered for a moment and then suddenly grabbed a blanket and threw it over the horse's head. He then asked the white man to tell the judges in which eye the horse was blind. The American was taken by surprise and blurted out that the horse was blind in his left eye. He had a fifty-fifty chance. The Indian then stated that the horse was not blind in either eye, a truth immediately recognized by everyone, as well as the dishonesty of the soldier and his comrades.

The commissioners had the soldier punished; they gave the horse and the soldier's saddle and accoutrements to the Indian. The Indian immediately took off the saddle and accoutrements and threw them at the feet of the soldier. He said he would never wish to use goods that were the property of a thief.

So what in the world did the Indians do that made the white man think they were wild animals? Milfort had some prime examples which he had seen firsthand during his twenty years of journeys throughout the tribes of the Creek Nation.

Milfort wrote that the Chickasaws had an unusual custom. When a warrior died, his wife was buried with him while she was still alive. The tribe would place both of them in a deep, narrow pit, and throw into it all his weapons of war and all their household utensils. They added some food provisions, and then they refilled the hole, thereby suffocating the wife. That would ensure that she would never leave her husband, and they would travel happy trails together forever. Through practices such as this, the Chickasaws became a weak, lightly-populated tribe, leading to their asking to join the Creek Nation. As a condition of joining the alliance, the general council of the Creeks pressured the Chickasaws to give up that barbaric practice, which they did.

The Choctaws were not very warlike; they were cowards, lazy and slovenly. They had good lands, but instead of farming, they preferred the life of beggars. They travelled to see the white Governor of Louisiana several times a year, begging for food. He would feed them for three days at government expense and then send them on their way.

The gratuity of provisions was voluntary on the part of the governor, but it generated into a habit the Indians regarded as obligatory. If the governor then refused to oblige, the Indians resorted to pillage and other acts of violence. At the end of the three days, they were sent back home with enough provisions to last them a week. On the way home, they would beg from the white settlers for corn and bread. They would make a porridge and eat it with fish they caught in the rivers, streams, and ponds along the way. They were very fond of horse flesh. They preferred it, even if the animal died of natural causes, to beef or any other meat.

The savages were so dirty and so lazy that they would never clean any part of their bodies. The young women tried to appear pretty by piercing the dividing membrane of their noses and passing a ring with a pendant through them. All the savages were very fond of those ornaments and wore them continuously.

Milfort witnessed the disturbing manner in which the Indians treated their dead. When a Choctaw died, his relatives built a scaffold twenty feet in front of his house, wrapped him in a buffalo or bear robe and left him up there for seven or eight months. Once the corpse was putrefied, their Indian priest climbed up and separated the bones and remaining flesh with his hands, leaving the flesh to burn and giving the bones to the deceased's relatives. Without washing his hands, the priest served the ceremonial meal of boiled horseflesh. Everyone ate and danced until all the food was gone, and then they went home.

The Choctaw priests or doctors were paid for treating their sick patients. When an illness lasted a long time and a Choctaw's assets ran out, the doctor called the family together and said that the illness was incurable. He told them the only humane thing to do was to put an end to his patient's suffering. Unfortunately, the sick man had seen this all before. One or two of the strongest family members were selected to go to the patient and ask how he was doing. While he was answering, the select family members would throw themselves on him and strangle him to death.

When any of the Indian tribes gathered together for any reason, they smoked their pipes before starting into business. They would also take a drink made from the leaves of a local wild tea tree. The leaves of the tree remained green all year, and they were picked only when needed.

At the assemblies, the leaves were roasted in a large bowl on a fire. When they dried, water was added and the mixture boiled. They filtered it and put it into earthenware pots. Once cooled, it was put into gourds and served to each of the members of the assembly.

After the Indian had taken his fill of the drink, he began to vomit, easily with no effort. Why would these savages make and drink this concoction if it were going to make them sick? The reason was simple. The drinking and vomiting ceremony had a great purpose in the events of an assembly. The purpose of the disgusting ceremony was to assure the chief of the assembly that each of the members who attended it had a stomach free of food or spirits and, consequently, a clear head. The chief would then be sure that all deliberations would be considered reasonably, and that strong liquor would not influence any assembly or tribal decisions. Wouldn't that be a great lesson for the civilized white man to follow?

The Creeks who populated the land along the route of the Georgia Rail Road were medium sized and copper colored. They were very strong and robust and could bear fatigue easily. Once mean and cruel, they were mild-mannered and brave from the 1800s on, unless they were provoked.

The Creeks recognized the Master of Breath, but they had no religious ceremonies of their own. Each year in the month of August, quite like the camp meetings of the whites, they assembled by settlements to celebrate the harvest festival. During the festival, the women threw out all worn-out household goods in anticipation of all new furnishings to be acquired during the new year. During the festival time, the Indians forgot and forgave all the causes of past and present quarrels. A savage who would recall an old quarrel after the festival was looked down upon by all the others.

When the Creeks prepared for war, each chief gave his men a drink they called the war medicine. The medicine was a liquor which had to be taken for three successive days before battle. The Indians knew for a fact that if they were surprised before the three days were finished, they would be defeated.

If the chief were defeated, which was sure to happen if his soldiers had no confidence, he would be responsible for anything that had happened. He would be accused of having caused the defeat due to his negligence in not distributing the war medicine on time. There were two kinds of medicine: the big and the small. The superstition was that the big medicine made the warrior invincible. The small medicine served to make the dangers of the fight seem smaller to the warrior. Warriors knew that if the chief offered him only the small medicine, then the fight was not going to be too rough, and that built up their confidence.

The medicine, which was really nothing to speak of, did help the chiefs in the time of war. One way was because the Indians loved to become intoxicated on strong liquor, and the chiefs had to find a way to keep them sober without upsetting them too much. The ruse worked because the Creeks were not allowed to take any liquor before taking the medicine, a matter which they religiously followed. The second positive result of taking the medicine was that it was the same vomit drink administered at the tribe assemblies. The warriors were purged by it, and any wounds they received in battle were in less danger of getting infected and healed rather quickly. The Creeks also decreased the danger of infections in battle because they fought almost naked. Woolen clothing, particles of which almost always remained in their wounds, made the wounds more difficult to heal, and, therefore, made the wounds more dangerous. Fighting naked eliminated the problem.

Muskogee Indians were like fire ants; they were peaceful and trouble-free until something provoked them. Fire ants leave you alone until they perceive that you may be trying to harm them or destroy their beds. The Muskogees acted the same. When a Muskogee killed a man, he cut off the skin from a large part of his head. These scalps did not all have the same worth; they were classified and judged by the chiefs who witnessed the feat. The greater the number of scalps taken and their individual merit determined the warrior's advancement in his military and civilian life. Most people have heard that the Spanish taught the Indians to scalp their enemies, but the Indians had used that practice prior to the Spanish to determine who was to be elevated to important positions in the tribe.

Since it was a great honor to kill the enemies of their tribe, each warrior claimed he had killed the most. To prove which warrior had actually killed the most, scalps had to be taken from the dead. A young Creek who, having been to war, did not bring back at least one scalp had to continue using the name of his mother and was unable to get a wife. When a young warrior brought back his first scalp, the chiefs of the assembly met him and gave him a name of his own. The chiefs determined the value of a scalp based on the dangers run to take it. The harder it was to take a scalp, the greater the value of it, and the greater the esteem of the warrior.

Most Indian tribes took no prisoners of war; they burned alive or horribly tortured to death any unfortunate enemies who happened to escape death on the battlefield. For both the victims and their executioners, it was a feast day. The winners rejoiced at the destruction of an enemy of their country, and the victims rejoiced over dying for his.

When Spanish priests tried to convert the Indians to Christianity in the early days of the meeting of the races, they had a terrible time changing them. One priest told the savages that to be the sons of God it was necessary for them to be the enemies of the Devil. The Indians would not accept that theory because, to them, the Devil was the best thing in the world; he made warriors brave and fearless.

The Franciscans stationed around the marshes of the sea islands of South Carolina resorted to using Indians as beasts of burden when all their horses eventually died. The Indians were forced to carry the friars' goods on their backs when they had to accompany them to visits to their substations. Rather than do that, many Indians rejected Christianity and resorted to old-fashioned barbarism. Many Indians were killed or died doing the work of the friars. So great was the horror of burden-carrying that many Indian women killed their offspring rather than see them become human carriers. So who were the savages and who were the civilized people?

12 Relocate Terminus, Sherman, Slavery, Impending Doom, and Bloody Tariffs

In 1841 and 1842, official company reports made references that Judge John P. King was a second Chief Engineer of the company. This obviously showed that Thomson's position and authority had been diminished. At the 1842 annual stockholders meeting, Thomson gave a controlled, conservative, dull report. He seemed a little depressed.

"Ladies and gentlemen, the enterprise as we had originally planned has been virtually completed. I know that sounds odd, because we still have miles of track to lay, but there will be no surprises which will hinder our connection to the state road. Our receipts are up for the year, and we have a six percent net return on our money. We are beginning to enjoy rail traffic from Alabama and Tennessee on the completed part of our line."

At this point, with such encouraging words, a motion was made from the floor to strike out any such discussion in any resolutions about discontinuing Thomson's services. Many people were on Thomson's side and wanted him to stay. The motion to support Thomson carried by more than two to one, about 12,000 to 5,000. Thomson was once again named as the company's only chief engineer. He had endured the storm and rededicated himself to the completion of the road.

Thomson brought up the question relative to the most advantageous power to be used on the railroad. He was undecided between the existing arrangement, which was a mix of light steam engines accompanied by horse power when needed, and a new improved machine to be developed by his friend Matt Baldwin. Thomson said that when the road begins to decay, steam power would have to be abandoned entirely. Light engines had been so inefficient that Thomson despaired of their success under any circumstances.

Thomson further stated, "Mr. Baldwin has offered to furnish an engine of the kind referred to, upon reasonable terms, which will not weigh more on the driving wheels, than is borne by either pair of wheels of our freight cars. As the purchase of such a machine would involve an expense, which under the present exigencies of the Company cannot be well incurred, I have left open for future decision permanent arrangements for conducting the business" of our road.

The Banner, published in Athens, on Friday, December 10, 1841, had reported that the Georgia Railroad had at length reached its termination at Athens. Though not completed, it was so far finished as to enable the company to forward passengers and goods through the whole length of the road. All that remained was to build turn outs at the end of the road, and erect a depot, both of which were in progress of construction. The exact date of the first train to Athens is not known, but it appears from this announcement that it was between December 1st and 10th, 1841.

Thomson, in the field with his construction engineers at the very end of 1842, forwarded a letter to the president. "Judge King, we have a problem. I have just received a report from Governor Schley. Chief Engineer Charles Garnett of the state road says that we can't place the terminal as originally laid out by Colonel Long. The area around the river where he had planned to end his road is entirely too sandy and is unsuitable for a terminal.

"The Governor has called for me as our Chief Engineer, Charles Garnett as Chief of the Western and Atlantic, and Foster Beckham, Chief of the Monroe Railroad, to meet and to decide on a suitable terminal. We will meet at Marthasville and solve this quickly. We will keep the stockholders of all three railroads in mind as far as costs and time elements are required."

Colonel Stephen Long was the Corps Engineer whom the Georgia Rail Road directors originally wanted as its Chief Engineer. As the Corps Engineer, he had been locating a road from Belfast, Maine, to Quebec. He unexpectedly took a leave of absence from the Corps and became the Chief Engineer for the new Western and Atlantic Railway of the State of Georgia. With a guaranteed salary of $5,000 per year from the state, he was eager to begin. He reported directly to the Governor. Colonel Long arrived in north Georgia in May of 1837. He had the entire line from Chattanooga to Terminus surveyed and his report submitted by November 3, 1839. The state route was laid almost exactly as he had recommended. His job done, he then promptly quit the Western and Atlantic at the end of 1840 and rejoined the Army Corps.

James S. Williams took over as Chief Engineer of the Western and Atlantic when Colonel Long resigned. Williams, an 1831 graduate of the United States Military Academy, fought Indians for six years before leaving the Army. He was in charge of Georgia's state road from the end of 1840 through early 1842. Williams reenlisted in the Army after leaving the Western and Atlantic. He spent the remainder of a long career in government positions in Florida, Arkansas, the Pacific Coast, and the Gulf of Mexico.

In February of 1842, Georgia's new Governor McDonald named prominent engineer Charles Fenton Mercer Garnett as the Chief Engineer to follow Mr. Williams. Garnett led the Western and Atlantic until December 1849. He subsequently enjoyed illustrious careers with the Memphis and Charleston Railroad, the Virginia and Tennessee Railroad, and several other smaller railroads. Mr. Garnett was the capable man who found the state road's problem with the terminal location.

Foster Beckham was a much respected Southern gentleman, soft spoken with a heart of gold. He was a fanatic on matters concerning railroads and steam engines. He was an astute businessman, but he was not a professional engineer of the caliber of Long or Thomson. He took the reins of the Monroe Railroad and Banking Company when it was charted in December of 1833. It opened with a well-built road from Macon to Forsyth, but the terrible economic depression of the Panic of 1837 sent it into bankruptcy in 1844.

The three men, Thomson, Garnett, and Beckham, were soon in agreement on setting the final meeting spot of their railroads. With the new terminal location definitely known and marked with a handsomely cut stone, the companies had only to complete the construction of their lines. The fire was put out and Thomson returned to Augusta.

Too busy with the work of the railroad and his many varied other investments, Thomson rarely allowed anyone to entertain him. But there were times when even Thomson could not politely turn down an invitation. Besides, he actually did want to see the inside of the Captain's Quarters at the Augusta Arsenal. As Thomson strolled through its grounds, he marveled at the magnificent headquarters building and its ornate white columns, a beautiful contrast to its yellow stucco walls. This building was the hub of the United States Army's brain-trust in the South.

The command, originally located near downtown in 1819, moved its operations three miles up to the Hill section of Augusta in 1827. The well-intended goal was to avoid the damp and vapid air of the flat, wet western side of town. However, the move did little to eliminate the effects of mosquitoes carrying yellow jack. The calm, cool fresh air on the Hill was a welcome relief in any event from the oppressive humidity of Augusta's summers.

Returning inside the columned building to join the festivities of the 1844 White Ladies' Ball, Thomson saw that the dance floor was crowded. The ladies had done a fine job of promotion and arm-twisting to get the gentry of Augusta up on the Hill. Thomson was accidently pushed into one of the Army officers who had been coerced into attending the Ball. The officer was a second lieutenant of the 3rd U. S. Artillery; he had been stationed at the Arsenal for almost the last two years. The young man's hair on his head was about the same length as his scruffy beard. His face was rough, sun-burned with deep rivulets running down his cheeks. He looked the part of the Indian fighter he had been since his graduation from West Point in 1840.

"Good evening, Lieutenant, please excuse my uncalled-for closeness, but fortune and this crowd have forced me upon you as it seems. But while I have your attention, how have you liked being stationed in this fine fortress?"

"And how are you, sir? No harm done, I hope I haven't spilled my drink on your lovely waistcoat. I have enjoyed my duty here fairly well to date, but I do long for getting back into the field where a military man can do his job," Lieutenant Sherman replied.

"I can certainly understand that; I, too, am consumed by a desire to get into my chosen field and to do my job quickly and efficiently, as I suspect you do. Let me introduce myself. I am Edgar Thomson, the Chief Engineer of the Georgia Railroad."

"Pleased to make your acquaintance, sir. My name is William Sherman, but friends call me Cump. Cump sounds kinda weird, but it comes from my middle name Tecumseh. I'm originally from Ohio, but I lived with my foster dad and family in Charleston. Dad is quite a politician, so I've been around the upper class of southern society for years, but I believe these ladies of Augusta take the cake. What a great job they've done this year."

"With your connections, I wonder why you didn't choose politics as a profession. Surely your father would have made it easy for you to become successful in it. How did you end up as an officer here in Augusta?" Thomson inquired.

"Well, I've always been kinda brusque with people. I have a temper at times and I certainly dislike the pomp and circumstance of politics. So, Dad and I thought maybe the military would mellow me. They always say the military will make the man.

"At the Academy I was not considered a good soldier. I was never selected for any office. I was just a private during my entire four years. I didn't like the spit and polish they demanded. It was always about neatness in dress and the strict conformity to their rules. That's what it took to be an officer, but I didn't excel in any of those.

"I was always respectable in my studies, and I did finish sixth in my graduating class. I would have been fourth except I had about one hundred and fifty demerits a year. After graduation, I was sent down to Florida to fight the Seminoles in the Second Seminole War, and then I was stationed here in this small border patrol.

"Hopefully, we're securing the frontier against the few hostile Indians still around. But, in truth, sir, we are really here to respond to any attempt that the people of South Carolina may make to secede from the Union over the nullification issues they have with the Black Tariff."

Thomson was intrigued with this young man who he guessed was maybe ten years younger than himself. He did have a fine up-right military bearing, and although his rough features and uncombed hair were totally opposite that of Thomson, he reminded Thomson of himself. However, in comparison with Thomson's carefully coiffured hair, Sherman's looked as if it had been cut by a five-year-old girl who had been playing with scissors.

"You said you were from Ohio. I am from Pennsylvania," Thomson said. "Let me ask you, how do you think this sectional animosity over slavery will conclude? Where do think this country is headed? Will we ever be able to agree on anything?" As one of the hostesses of the ball walked up with a tray of cool refreshments, Sherman took one and offered another to Thomson. Thomson hardly ever drank alcoholic beverages, but he didn't want to appear stiff-necked or too prudish like the Quaker he had been raised to be, so he accepted the drink.

"Thank you. So what does a young military man from Ohio who was raised in the cradle of Southern hospitality and charm feel about this peculiar institution?"

Sherman paused a moment before he answered. He wanted to be sure he could trust his true feelings with this new acquaintance. "My brother John is a staunch anti-slavery congressman, but I don't share his deep feelings about slavery. I am, in fact, sympathetic to these Southerners' defense of their system.

"People have a right to govern themselves according to the Constitution. That 'three-fifths of all other Persons' phrase the framers put in the Constitution sums it all up for me. If 'all men are created equal' is correct like the Declaration of Independence states, and if it refers to all men, red and black and white, why did our founders have to put that 'three-fifths of all other Persons' in there?

"I've thought about it often. 'All men are created equal' was our founders' way of telling the British that we would suffer death before we would have a government in this country that had Lords and Ladies, Kings and Queens, Princes and Princesses. All free white and black American men are equal under the law, but they are not physically created equal.

"I agree that all men should definitely be equal under the laws of the land. But the 'men' referred to in the Declaration were the common men of England, who had been the King's subjects while living in the Colonies, but who were now Americans. These were men, both black and white, who were independent and free, hard-working men who wanted a voice in running the affairs of their government.

"We had had enough of England's House of Lords, filled with its rich, arrogant dandies waltzing around London in their fine robes and silly wigs, bowing to the King and Queen. They are no better than we common people are. If we wanted a King, we would have demanded that George Washington become our King.

"We didn't want a House of Commons, either. Hell, we're all commoners in this country. Each man for himself; no one higher than another by birth. That's the secret; no one higher than another just because someone says he has royal or special blood. I don't care what that person says his mother or father did. What matters is what he himself does.

"Our Constitution states that representatives and direct taxes would be apportioned to the individual states of the union, determined by adding to the whole number of free men of each state, no Indians, and three-fifths of all other persons. The way I see it, we had three categories of men mentioned: free men, both black and white, men who were bound to another under slavery, and Indians. Nowhere in the Declaration or the Constitution is there a reference to women. At the time of our Revolution, women had the same status that they had in the England they just left, or even in the Bible; none. It would be a sad day to me if women became the equal to men and, heaven forbid, even got the right to vote. It goes without saying that I feel the same way about the Indians."

Mr. Sherman looked casually around, making sure no one was listening to his conversation. He began to tell Thomson how he really felt about the deplorable state of American political affairs. He did not want to be drawn into a shouting match, or possibly a duel, by a spectator over his next remarks.

"But whenever I hear some rebel-rouser getting beside himself, talking about disunion and secession, I have always said that I sympathize with him but I oppose any attempt at dissolving our union. I tell him that the people of the South don't know what they're doing. This country will be drenched in blood. God only knows how it will end.

"I tell them it is all folly, madness, a crime against civilization! Those people talk so lightly of war, but they don't know what they're talking about. War is a terrible thing. They mistake, too, the people of the North. They are a peaceable people, but do not be deceived, they will fight. They are not going to let this country be destroyed without a fight to preserve it.

"Besides, where are the men and the weapons of war to contend against them? The North can make a steam engine, a locomotive, or railway car. Mr. Thomson, you know that even more than I do. I tell the discontents that the people here can hardly make a yard of cloth or a pair of shoes. The South is rushing into war with one of the most powerful, ingeniously mechanical, and determined people on Earth.

J. EDGAR THOMSON, THE GEORGIA RAIL ROAD YEARS, 1833 – 1845

"The South is bound to fail. Only in their spirit and their determination are they prepared for war. In all else, they are totally unprepared for war, and they have a bad cause, too. At first they will make headway, but as their resources begin to fail, shut out from the markets of Europe as they will be, their cause will begin to wane.

"If the people here will just stop and think, they must see that in the end, they will surely fail. I apologize for preaching to you, Mr. Thomson, but I think that what I've said is what every Southerner should hear and heed. I may only be a lowly lieutenant in this man's army, but I think I have a pretty good feel for the state of things. I only hope that I'll never have to come back down here as the enemy of the South. I really do think war is hell, but I'll do whatever duty calls me to do."

"Well said, Lieutenant. You certainly have a way with words. I think you'll go far, if not in the military, maybe you really should reconsider entering politics. If these Southerners had enough strong willed leaders who opposed secession, maybe the future would be brighter. I agree with you, however, that the states should be able to govern themselves. That right is the cornerstone of our Constitution.

"As it says in that magnificent document which will live forever in this country, unsullied by any person or political party, we are the 'united' States of America, with a little U. From the beginning we were separate but equal states, drawn together only temporarily to fight our common foe, England, for our freedom. We banded together and did defeat England, but that time has passed. We were never the 'United' States, with a capital U, one entire nation to be governed as a Federal or Central government.

"I believe in states' rights, and I wish that the politicians of the North did, too. But I will tell you the truth: there are two groups of people I do not trust in any capacity, lawyers and politicians. I do hope there is time to heal the hatred between the North and the South before an actual war comes, because I believe you are perfectly correct in your assessment. The South will be doomed.

"You mentioned the Black Tariff earlier. I can tell you it's killing us. Everything I buy for my railroad from England, including finished goods and raw materials, now costs me more than forty percent higher than I could buy it without the tariff.

"You may not know, having been in the field fighting Indians, about the additional costs all of us have to pay so that the Northern industries can make more profits. The tariff has been charged since 1816. It was increased in 1824 and again in 1832, when it reached its high point."

"Who pushed for the tariffs? How did they come about?" Sherman asked.

"Well, the main goal of the tariffs was to protect industries in the North. They were having financial problems up there due to the influx of low-priced goods from England. Southern planters were buying most of their finished goods from England. To make Americans buy Northern goods, every time a European product was purchased, we had to pay a forty percent tax on it. It made the Northern goods competitive.

"So, if a businessman had a product he was buying that actually cost $1,000, he had to pay $1,400 for it. That extra $400 on each transaction could put him out of business. Our railroad buys many tons of iron products a year from England, and we have enough financial problems of our own without the tariff.

"The Southern merchants protested, and their politicians forced a couple of compromises to give them a little relief, but two years ago President Tyler signed that Black Tariff of 1842 putting back that old forty percent tax on everything imported.

"What makes me sick is that the main beneficiary of the tariff protection is the iron industry. Import duties on both raw and manufactured iron goods amounts to about two-thirds of their entire cost to me. So if an item should cost, let's say, $90 to me without the tariff, and the Feds add two-thirds of that, or $60, as a tax, I have to pay $150 for it. It's disgusting and unfair.

"On nails and hoop iron we have to pay more than one hundred percent of their pre-tariff cost. And this new Black Tariff raises the different categories of goods it taxes from fifty percent to eighty-five percent of all imports. Hard to believe, eighty-five percent of all imported goods today have that tax.

"The people of the South hate the way everything from the Federal government is forced down their throats. Many of them want out of the so-called Union. They actually believe what the Constitution says about states' rights. And I agree with them.

"Unfortunately, not everyone else agrees. I've met with Andy Jackson two times, both in business matters. He once told me a story that happened when he was arguing with some South Carolina politicians over their anti-tariff resolutions. He said that in 1832 those men called on their fellow Carolinians to decide if they were going to tamely surrender their liberties without a struggle, or not.

"The implication was armed conflict between South Carolina and the Federal government. Jackson told me that he told the politicians to tell their people that they would be sorry to take up arms against the rest of the country. He said that they could talk and write resolutions to their hearts' content. But if one drop of blood was shed in the Carolinas in defiance of the laws of the United States, he would personally hang the first man of them he could get his hands on to the first tree he could find."

"What happened? What did South Carolina do?" asked Lt. Sherman.

"Well, John C. Calhoun told Jackson personally that the states had entered the Union of their own free will, and had retained the right to leave it at any time. Any state at any time. Jackson responded by writing his 'Proclamation to the People of South Carolina.'

"Jackson wrote that no state had the right to annul a Federal law. The people and not the states had formed the Union. To say that any state may secede at will from the Union is like saying that the United States is not a nation. He told the Nullifiers that disunion by armed force is an act of treason. Jackson then pushed through Congress his Force Bill, called the

Bloody Bill in South Carolina. The bill strengthened the military posts around South Carolina to enable them to use military force to collect the hated tariff duties. And that is why you're here, young man.

"One other thing you may find interesting is that the primary leader against the Force Bill was South Carolina's Governor, George McDuffie. The funny thing is that McDuffie was born in Frogpond, one of our railroad stops, and went on to become a national and a South Carolina political powerhouse. He is called the Great Nullifier and the Great Orator in all the newspapers, even up North. Look out for him. He comes to Augusta and Athens and Hamburg quite often. One day when you're not on duty, you should try to attend one of his rallies. He'll lecture for a couple of hours, and you'll love it. He could win a debate with the Devil himself."

Scotsman John McDuffie and his wife Jane had moved to America about 1780. They settled in the pine hills of present-day McDuffie County, Georgia, half-way between Frogpond and Lombardy. They became fast friends with Cap' Wilson and his family. The McDuffies were better educated than their neighbors, but they never made that an issue.

In 1790, George McDuffie was born. He worked as a farm-laborer from ten to twelve, and then became a clerk in James Calhoun's Augusta store, Calhoun and Wilson. Calhoun had met the red-headed boy on a trip to see Cap' Wilson, and decided the boy's potential needed a stimulus. McDuffie moved into Gus Longstreet's mother's boarding house in downtown Augusta and roomed with Longstreet in the attic. The Calhoun and Wilson business venture failed, and Calhoun's brother William came to Augusta from South Carolina to help close things out.

William Calhoun, impressed by McDuffie's intelligence, took George home with him and enrolled him in Moses Waddell's remarkable school in Willington, South Carolina. George was the number one student there, and graduated with Gus Longstreet in 1811. George went to the South Carolina College where he was also the best student, and Gus went to Yale. George delivered the valedictory speech at commencement in December of 1813.

McDuffie was soon considered one of the best lawyers in South Carolina, but, as all lawyers are wont to do, he entered the political arena. While in the U. S. House of Representatives, McDuffie wrote an anonymous series of letters to the *Georgia Gazette* criticizing Colonel William Cumming, a political opponent. Cumming demanded the name of the author, and the paper obliged. Cumming, an expert marksman, forced McDuffie into a duel over the letters. In June of 1822, their first duel took place at Tuck-a-see-king, or Sister's Ferry, on the South Carolina side of the Savannah River across from Augusta. McDuffie, probably scared to death, fired his ball into the ground midway between the duelers. Cumming then shot McDuffie through a rib, and the ball bounced around inside McDuffie until it lodged near his spine. The ball was never removed because of its dangerous position, but McDuffie survived the injury. During the aftermath of the duel, both men called the other a coward in public. A second planned duel arising from that name-calling was set to begin in North Carolina when law authorities stopped it. North Carolina had passed a dueling code forbidding duels twenty years earlier, and Cumming was arrested. The unfinished second duel was then moved to Lovers' Lane near the river at Augusta in October of 1822. Cumming's shot was right on the mark. The ball passed through McDuffie's body and on its exit, broke his left arm. McDuffie seemed not to be too greatly handicapped by his wounds for another twenty years, but then he began to lose all control of his legs. Not long after, he also lost the use of his limbs, and then he became totally immobile. When he died in 1851, he couldn't move and his mind was a complete blank. Such are the fruits of Satan's games.

As a handsome, dignified older man approached, Thomson spoke clearly so that both men could hear. "And here is my dear friend, Judge Benjamin Warren, who has caught us talking insurrection in this quaint old Southern military arsenal. Ben, I would like to introduce you to an amazing young lieutenant, William Sherman. Lt. Sherman, meet my friend, Judge Warren, who is the most respected mover and shaker in this town. Ben, I hope you won't file formal charges against us; we were only getting acquainted."

As the White Ladies' Ball wound down for another year, a pretty young lady walked up and took Thomson by the hand. "Excuse me, gentlemen, but Mr. Thomson has been owing me this dance all night. I know he is a charter member of the Georgia Railroad Bachelors' Club, but it is my duty as a hostess to see if we can't thaw his frosty opinion of womanhood and get Mr. Thomson on the dance floor. Who knows, he might just like it."

Thomson did, but the demands of the love of his life, his railroad, had much deeper talons wrapped around his mind than the girl's pretty young face and exquisite figure. "Well, Miss, I just might like it. You seem to be quite a piece of work. Tell me about yourself. Where are you from?"

"I was born in a little hamlet in Pennsylvania, near Pittsburgh," she answered. "My real name is JoAnn, but my friends call me JoJo. Please do the same."

"Well, I know quite well where Pittsburgh is, you know I was born in a little town outside Philadelphia myself. How in the world did you get down here? Married to a soldier?" Thomson replied.

"Well, he was a sailor, but you were close. He was killed fighting Seminoles during a raid on one of their villages. He was from here, and I stayed here because I like the city. His mother is like the mother I didn't have; mine died when I was five. I don't think I could ever go back to that cold, gloomy place up North. But, it's a long story. If I tell you the whole thing, you may have to buy me breakfast in the morning," she laughed.

Thomson gave her a long, hungry look and whispered in her ear, "Call me Edgar, my dear. I'd be delighted to buy you some breakfast in the morning, or I can make you some."

13 Early Passenger Travel, The Marietta Party, and The Augusta Canal

Early in 1845, Thomson sent word to the Board. "Gentlemen, the end is in sight. I have approved the opening of the road to Covington. All the grading and bridging is done except for the bridge over the Yellow River. We have some obstacles there, but we will deal with them quickly.

"We are a little inconvenienced by having to unload our rails from our cars and load them onto wagons. We then cross the river downstream, cut back to the road on the other side, and load them aboard another rail car. It's a small irritant, but we're getting the job done."

Thomson and his crews were certainly getting the job done. The road from Augusta to Madison was actively being used every day by passengers heading due west to Alabama. The most popular route from Augusta to Montgomery was via the so-called Monroe Railroad Line.

The railroad's billing stated that passengers would travel part of their journey by four-horse Post coaches until connecting with one of the Georgia, the Monroe, or the Montgomery and West Point Railroads. On trips originating in Augusta, the passengers and their luggage would first board the Georgia Railroad car to Madison.

At Madison, passengers continuing to Montgomery were transferred with their luggage to a four-horse stagecoach to continue to Macon. Passengers staying in Madison or going elsewhere would also disembark, going wherever they so desired. New passengers would climb aboard.

Arriving in Macon, the folks heading farther west boarded the Monroe Railroad's train from Macon to Forsyth. Some passengers disembarked in Macon and some new ones boarded. At Forsyth, the people heading to Montgomery were transferred once again to a fine stagecoach which took them to West Point. When the four-horse stagecoach reached West Point, the passengers continuing would finally board a train, thankfully for the last time, and head nonstop in relative comfort to Montgomery.

The entire journey included 171 miles by train, the rest by stage. From Augusta to Madison the trip cost $5.25. From Madison to Macon it cost $6.00. From Macon to Montgomery the trip set you back $21.00. The entire trip from Augusta to Montgomery would cost a passenger $32.25, which was quite expensive for an ordinary man making $300 a year. There were no discounts for straight through service. The total travel time was only fifty hours. Food and bed were optional or nonexistent. What was it like to travel those two solid days in wind and dust, in freezing cold or blazing heat, pushed up against a stranger who had missed his Saturday bath, had not brushed his teeth and had never heard of deodorant? It must have been similar to being a member of Moses' horde walking forty years through desert sand without water for personal or sanitary hygiene.

The Reverend Adiel Sherwood in his 1829 edition of his *Gazetteer* gave the stagecoach fares for numerous trips. For the fare from Augusta to Charleston he said the rate was "$15.00 and found." Without having been a passenger on a stagecoach journey, it is hard to understand what that means.

With all the transferring from stage to rail, and rail to stage, some people were actually lost during their journey. It's understandable; it was all fairly new, the roads were terrible, it was hot, or cold, or dusty. Passengers were tired, dirty, and disgusted. Who wouldn't get confused? Higher rates were charged on some burdensome routes because the fare included the cost of finding the missing passenger. That was being "found." The quoted fare ensured that the coach's patron would eventually complete his journey and would be fed at no cost the entire time he was travelling. It was like paying for travel insurance.

During their trips through Georgia in the 1800s, passengers could find several decent places to stay, but on a trip from Augusta to Montgomery, the only decent places were in Augusta, Macon, Forsyth, West Point and Montgomery. Arriving at a hotel, passengers would find the office in a corner of the main room, or lobby, so to speak.

After signing in, the new arrivals now had a bedroom and a key. The room had all the necessities of life — a bed, a lamp, a dresser, a desk, and a chair. Nailed to the back of the door was a schedule of meal times and other minor bits of trivia. There was no trouble ordering dinner; travelers came and went just as they pleased. They could generally eat during the posted hours, if they so desired. It wasn't mandatory, but it was smart. If they missed the prepared dinner, heaven forbid what they may be eating after posted dinner hours. One group of attorneys attending court in Madison all stayed at the only hotel in town. The same whole hog, without the benefit of refrigeration, graced the dinner table the entire four days of their business trip.

Each room had a little pigeonhole on the office desk where passengers could see if they had mail awaiting them. As primitive as it may seem, the luxury of a hot meal and then a pitcher of hot water on your desk in your room was something to be remembered. Baths were available for anyone who might have needed one after forty or fifty hours on the road, even on an evening other than a Saturday.

For passengers heading south from Augusta or Hamburg to Savannah, and from there to the rest of the world, another mode of travel was available. The era of steamboating had begun. With steam power, men were able to travel at ease against the current. Some of the steamboats were elegantly decked out to impress their passengers; others were drab but functional. Some were floating palaces covered with wooden scrollwork, while some were dangerous wooden apartments waiting for disaster on the river.

In the better steamboats, the cabins were splendid, decked out in mahogany. Their style, their splendor, their quietness far exceeded that of any local tavern. You read, you talked, you relaxed, and you slept, as you chose.

The more common passenger vessels on the Savannah were filthy and the fare was worse. The passengers consisted of Crackers, Gougers, planters, business men, drunkards, and gamblers, and their ladies and children of the same sort. They had to dip the water for washing from the river in tin basins, that is, if they cared about their aroma or appearance.

They had to soap themselves all from the same cake of soap, and the entire passenger list wiped with the same solitary towel, rolled over a pin to extract a little of its dirty water. The towel would have been hard to determine if it were manufactured of hemp, flax, or cotton.

The steamer's beds had two sheets that were two and a half feet wide. The pillows would have been filled with corn-shucks or goose feathers. When it rained outside, it also rained inside. At that time the ladies would scream, the babies would squall, and the dogs would yell. And through it all, it still beat spending five days in a stagecoach.

Addressing the many questions running through his mind before the linkup with the state road, Edgar Thomson sent a communique to the Board. "Gentlemen, I have heard through the grapevine that the Western and Atlantic, for whatever reason, has not thought to purchase a locomotive. If we are to partner, in effect, with them and to be a link in the Western and Atlantic connection with them, then I feel we must be cooperative with them in our operations.

"I am sure if our old friend Colonel Long had not left the W & A and reentered the Corps of Engineers this would never have happened. The state legislature should investigate the cause of this negligence. I hope this will not be a sign of the future in our dealings with them. In any event, gentlemen, please entertain the thought of lending them one of our engines until theirs has arrived, if indeed they have ordered one.

"I will discuss this with Chief Garnett if you approve, and then I will make the loan proposal to him if you agree. I do not want to embarrass him until I have your permission to approach him on the subject. He is an honorable man, but if this situation is due to negligence, there will be no one to blame except Mr. Garnett. However, there is the real possibility that the state has not agreed with him to purchase one at this time. Sometimes it would be better if politicians would not be allowed to make business decisions like this."

By August of 1845, the track had reached Decatur, just six miles east of Marthasville, the end of the road. The Western and Atlantic road had reached its final destination at the White Hall Tavern, six miles west of the Chattahoochee River. It was called White Hall Tavern because it was the only real building in one hundred miles, and its proprietor had painted it white.

In September of 1845, the last loose rail on the Georgia Railroad was spiked onto its nine-inch wooden stringer. That rail was then bolted to its sister rail on the Western and Atlantic, connecting the two railroads. (On April 13, 1859, President King reported that the road from Washington to Athens would be relaid with a light T rail on cross-ties, the first use of them.) On September 11, 1845, the first train, loaded with local political and railroad company officials from Augusta, arrived at Atlanta, as it was now called. There were several congratulatory speeches and toasts made there to celebrate the finish of the great undertaking. Backs were slapped and hands were shaken.

Grand opening festivities were planned, but not there in Atlanta. The excitement and partying would come elsewhere. Since there were only six buildings and thirty residents in Atlanta, it was not the location suitable for a gala event such as Thomson had in mind. Marietta, however, was, and it was not far up the road across the Chattahoochee on the Western and Atlantic line. Marietta had become a fine, booming city on the rise, and it was chosen as the best place for the party.

After the speeches, Thomson went up into the cab and spoke with the locomotive's engineer. He had to speak directly into his ear so he could be heard over the hissing of the engine. "Mr. Adair, you and Mr. Hardman pull us on the side track and let's get this engine cleaned and polished while we have time. It looks like you still have plenty of steam."

"I have spoken too soon. Time has definitely slipped up on us," Thomson said a little later to Mr. Adair. "This engine takes a lot longer to spruce up than one would think. We'll just have to spend the night here and set out at first light tomorrow. Would you be so kind as to get someone to ride over to the Western and Atlantic folks and tell them that we'll meet them tomorrow morning? With my apologies."

Some of the dignitaries found shelter in the few buildings in Atlanta, some slept in the passenger car and some slept on the ground. Others stayed up all night enjoying the local refreshments provided by the fine residents of Atlanta. Most of those who couldn't sleep, partied and lounged around the half-finished brick depot beside the tracks. One state official sitting outside thanked a man handing him a jug, "First time I've had moonshine while sitting in the moonshine. Thanks, and to your health, young sir. Umm, this stuff is good. This is some well-made sipping whisky. Have a seat, young man, and tell me about yourself."

"Well, sir, I was raised right here, down that road about five miles. My old granddad lives with me and my dad. Granddad's seventy-seven and dad's forty. Dad got married young, so I'm already twenty-two. Mom died two months ago in a buggy accident. She was coming home from the Widow Thomas' house in a driving rain in the middle of the night and was blown off the road. She never let any of us go with her on her visits to the needy, and the storm was unexpected and came up quickly.

"Mom had gone to deliver the Widow's bastard son. The poor thing died two days later from malnutrition. The Widow was bad off, too, and died a month after giving birth. She was in worse shape than the baby. People say she was mentally ill, but I know what her illness really was.

"I sold her a gallon or more of this shine each week for the last five years. That was her mental illness. But, I guess if I was a whore, I'd drink like a fish, too. But she had to support herself somehow. My mother was a lovely lady with yellow hair and blue eyes. Her kindness took her away from us, and we miss her something fierce."

"Sorry, son. Tell me about this shine, as you call it," said the official. "How do you make it?"

"Well, there ain't much to it. You heat up some good, clear brook water, stir in your corn mash, and add some sugar and yeast. When it starts cooling, the vapors run through a pipe and turn to a liquid. That's your shine. Everybody round here makes shine, so we name our own product. I call mine Mash 4077. That's because it's made with corn mash, and my dad is forty and granddad is seventy-seven."

"That name sounds familiar. I must have heard it in Milledgeville," said the state official.

William Hardman, the locomotive engineer on this first train to Atlanta, in an interview in *The Augusta Chronicle* in 1885, related this true story. The locomotive-and-one-car train took off for Marietta on the new state road the next morning, just as soon as the passengers could shake the kinks and cobwebs from their persons. When they reached the Chattahoochee River, Thomson and his Philadelphia friend, Richard Peters, got out to inspect the tracks over the bridge. The two men walked ahead with Engineer Hardman and found that the Western and Atlantic gandy dancers in their hurry had neglected to secure two rails.

"There's no justification for anything like this to ever happen. I am truly disappointed in the disgraceful lack of diligence of their engineers in the inspection of this bridge. Let's get some men and equipment and fix this right now. And get some spikes if they're missing. Someone has got to answer for this when we get to Marietta."

The passengers had been taking a long, close look at what had happened, and they left the train in a hurry. Thomson and Peters and the engine crew walked the train across the bridge when the track was operational, and the passengers quietly followed.

"If we had tried to cross the river last night, we would have all ended up in the Chattahoochee. We would have all been killed. We went out at first light. We had no head-lights, we couldn't see anything in the early darkness. We had no whistle, no cow-catcher, and no cab. The engineer stood on the engine's platform without shelter of any kind. The maximum speed of our train was twelve miles per hour." Mr. Hardman made the first cow-catcher ever used on a train.

Thomson had always tried to remain calm when faced with an unpleasant situation. But once he was fully apprised of any negative situation, he took action. He left no doubt as to how he felt when he accosted the officials of the state road. He put them on notice that their lack of concern in overseeing their road could possibly end his semi-partnership cooperation with their road.

He told the Western and Atlantic men, including Mr. Garnett, that he would give Governor Crawford a complete report on what had transpired. The Governor, thrown by his horse in Milledgeville two days earlier, had been unable to attend the festivities, much to his regret.

Thomson had especially thanked Governor Crawford for his support for the railroads during his term in office. Crawford had been instrumental in providing the funds needed to complete the state road from Chattanooga to Marthasville. He had cleared all legal issues of both the state road and the Georgia Railroad quickly and in almost all cases to the benefit of the roads. Born in Columbia County, Georgia, George W. Crawford was elected to two terms as governor. He served in many capacities in state and national agencies and was the Secretary of War under President Zachary Taylor. His better-known cousin was William Harris Crawford, presidential candidate in 1824.

The Augustans returned home in their little passenger car. Four days later, on September 15, 1845, the railroad was officially opened and regular train service began over the entire line from Atlanta to Augusta. An 1845 advertisement in an Augusta newspaper gave the public a timetable with pricing for the trip from Augusta to Atlanta.

The train left Augusta at 8:00 p.m. sharp and arrived in Atlanta around 7:30 a.m. It was one passenger train, one way, each night, and then at 8:00

a.m. it returned on the reverse time schedule. For $7.00 one could travel the 171 miles uninterrupted in eleven and a half hours. Children under twelve and Negroes travelled for half fare.

Each passenger was allowed 112 pounds of luggage. Union Point, seventy-six miles from Augusta, was the only stop for refreshments during the trip. The only item of promotion on the 1845 advertisement was to let all travelers to Augusta know that the United States Hotel, kept by Daniel Mixer, had excellent accommodations. It also provided a good table of food and had the most attentive servants.

One would think Thomson would go home and relax after the highly successful Marietta party, but he had many commitments and naturally would not rest until they were fulfilled.

Many events concerning Augusta's economy and growth were having an impact on the city. Back in 1840, when the Georgia Railroad wasn't finished and economic times were terrible, the South Carolina Canal and Rail Road Company, which ran from Charleston to Hamburg, offered financial help for the state of Georgia. The catch was that the Georgians had to grant a charter to allow the South Carolina railroad to cross the river into Georgia from Hamburg into Augusta.

Augusta businessmen did not want the economic competition and heartily persuaded the state and local politicians to not grant them one, and they didn't. The business folks didn't want any new business around that would make them lower the very profitable rates they were charging.

Mayor Martin Dye called a civic meeting in 1841 to form a Home Industry Society which would provide work for those women who needed it. The society solicited money to buy materials that the women could make into saleable home-made goods. The society eventually had a hundred women on its payroll, and Augustans were mercifully buying their home-spun products. Unfortunately, the venture failed in 1843, and the remaining monies were given directly to the poor and needy. Something had to be done to rescue the city.

In September of 1844, Thomson had received an invitation for dinner at the home of Henry and Julia Cumming. He naturally assumed it was merely a congratulatory barbeque of some sort. Mr. Cumming was a lifelong Augustan who was involved in every stage of the city's affairs. His father served as Augusta's first mayor after its incorporation. His brother was the first non-Mormon governor of the Utah Territory.

Cumming had been worrying over the dreadful effects of the economic downturn of the 1840s, particularly to Augusta and the South, and envisioned building a canal to stimulate Augusta's economy. Located on the Savannah River, Augusta had been the ideal place to receive and accumulate the planters' cotton heading down the river to Savannah and on to England. The collapse of cotton prices during the depression of 1837 left Augusta in terrible economic shape.

Cumming believed that the power generated from a canal would enable Augusta to set up a manufacturing base and diversify its economy. He thought Augusta could compete eventually with the industry of the North. Cumming's planter friends knew only one thing: planting. They dismissed Cumming's vision as a waste of time and money. But Henry Cumming was so confident in the success of his idea that he offered Edgar Thomson $500 of his personal funds as good faith that very night if Thomson would make the initial survey of the canal site.

At this time, the railroad was only months away from being opened from Augusta to Marthasville, but Thomson still had the personal time to accept Cumming's offer. He certainly didn't need the money, but Cumming's enthusiasm appealed to Thomson and he was genuinely touched by Cumming's dedication to an idea in which he truly believed. It seemed to be a quick and easy engagement.

After Thomson accepted the offer, Cumming next approached Augusta surveyor William Phillips to work hand-in-hand with Thomson. Thomson surprisingly took Phillips at face value in their working partnership. The engagement called for determining how much the water from the Savannah River would fall as it flowed from the beginning of its navigable waters downstream to downtown Augusta.

All through the winter of 1844, from Bulls Sluice to Hawk's Gulley, or Water's Edge, on Augusta's west side, the two surveyors and crews ran lines paralleling the Savannah River. It was apparent that the fifty-two foot drop over the six surveyed miles would provide plenty of power for the proposed project.

Cumming paid Thomson personally for his initial work, but didn't want to fund the whole project. He gathered the business and civic leaders of the area at a public meeting in January of 1845. He spoke to the crowd, "My fellow keepers of the dream for a prosperous Augusta and surrounding areas, thank you for meeting here tonight on this special occasion.

"It makes my heart glad to see that so many of my esteemed friends and other community leaders have taken the time and have the interest to investigate a project which has been dear to me for years. You have the results of the initial survey from Mr. Thomson and Mr. Phillips for the proposed canal in front of you. If not, there are some up here on this desk. Please get one and look at it. The engineering drafts and the rough estimated costs to construct the canal based on their observations are in there. I'm requesting help tonight for funds to complete the permanent survey by the two engineers."

Comments and a little skepticism abounded. No one ventured any pledge of funds for quite a while. Finally, William D'Antignac, the president of the Bank of Augusta, spoke up and made the first pledge. John P. King, the president of the Georgia Railroad and Banking Company, made the next pledge. Before the night was over, the four Augusta banks had pledged $4,000 to get the permanent survey done.

John Pendleton King was a great personal friend of Edgar Thomson's. Therefore, it comes as no surprise that he not only pledged bank funds for the canal, but also for its future support in any way. With the Georgia Railroad's backing, everyone knew nothing would go wrong.

Judge King was a U. S. Senator from Georgia from 1833-1837. He graduated from the illustrious Academy of Richmond County and studied law.

Admitted to the bar in 1819, he practiced in Augusta, went to Europe to study from 1822-1824, and returned to continue his practice in Augusta until 1829.

Being an influential lawyer in his early thirties, he was, of course, drawn into politics. In the 1830s, he was a member of two state constitutional conventions, a judge, and a U. S. senator. When he resigned his Senate seat in 1837, he was succeeded by Wilson Lumpkin; the same Wilson Lumpkin who inspired the names of Lumpkinville and Marthasville at the terminus of the Georgia Railroad.

After he satisfied his penchant for politics, King became the president of the Georgia Railroad and Banking Company from 1841 to 1878. It is obvious why he and Thomson were fast friends. Not only did they complete the railroad together, but they were involved with each other in many side investments, usually of great profit to each of them.

With money in hand, Thomson and Phillips began their survey. Thomson's father had supervised the construction of Philadelphia's Delaware and Chesapeake Canal. Thomson had carefully watched him do it, so he knew what needed to be done. Thomson chose to build a dam all the way across the Savannah River from Georgia to South Carolina. An opening on one side allowed the water to rush into the canal at its upper level. The water level would be only about five feet deep for this first level, which was almost the entire length of the canal.

Towards the end of the first level, two more levels were built parallel to the first. The water in the first level would service industries there and then drop thirteen feet into level two. From level two the water would fall thirteen more feet through mill power machinery into level three. Finished as a source of power, the water was diverted to the river via Beaver Dam Creek and Hawk's Gulley.

The City of Augusta issued $100,000 in bonds to finance the canal's construction. Due to some unusual complexities in the structuring of the bonds, the state legislature held up issuing a charter for the canal until December of 1845. Engineer O. C. Stanford agreed to complete the canal in one year for $2,500. Unfortunately for everyone, it took two.

Stanford used Thomson's plan for construction and organized it into twelve sections. All twelve sections were put out for bid. Judge Benjamin Warren took the first sections, numbers six and seven which ran through his soon-called Fruitland plantation. He was personally overseeing the clearing of the grade by May of 1846. James Coleman, Warren's brother-in-law, took sections four and five and had his crew of ten slaves working by May 2nd. The remaining sections were taken by the Georgia Railroad, using railroad construction methods there. The work was done. Warren, Coleman, and the Railroad had paid the costs for completing their sections and had been paid back through the use of the city's bond issue.

The canal's water first flowed on November 23, 1846. Cumming's dream had almost been fulfilled. The only problem was no manufacturing took place. The Augusta Manufacturing Company had been built, but no manufacturing was done due to bickering and confusion.

Finally, a search turned up Jacobez Smith, who took over management of the mill, and then things began to happen. Smith had come from Petersburg, Virginia and had worked in the mill business there for years. He knew what to do. The canal was a great success at last and Augusta's business took off. Thomson continued to work under contract with the Canal Commission and the City of Augusta whenever he was needed.

14 Goodbye Georgia Rail Road and Hello Pennsylvania Rail Road

In a Georgia Railroad Board meeting in July of 1846, nearly a year after regular train service began, Edgar Thomson said, "Gentlemen, the road is now completely finished. I commend you on providing and raising the funds to cover all $3,370,000 of our costs. Athens is now connected to Augusta, and Augusta is now connected to the Georgia state road.

"It has been my good fortune to have worked with you gentlemen. It has also been twelve long, hard years of backbreaking work. Overseeing the construction of a railroad in the crushing heat and the bitter cold, and sleeping in tents and in shacks, can quickly make a young man old. But the wonderful days and evenings I spent in Augusta in all the comforts of a fine metropolitan city of culture and refinement have been wonderful. I will never forget these days or the great friends I have made here.

"I envision a time in which I shall ride a train from the Atlantic to the Pacific without a change of cars. It may take three months to make such a trip, but it will be a glorious event in the history of our country and our magnificent railroad systems. I have had this vision constantly since I was a young boy in Pennsylvania. I am putting you on notice today that I will soon decide what changes I will have to make to fulfill that dream.

"The Georgia Railroad cannot satisfy my dream. She cannot go east, the Charleston and Hamburg road is there. She cannot go west, the

Western and Atlantic state road is there. As far as I can see, she has lost her potential to grow unless a line is run to Savannah or possibly to Charlotte. I want to build a railroad that will go west until it reaches the very shores of the Pacific Ocean."

John Edgar Thomson completed his Georgia Railroad from Augusta to Atlanta in 1845. Its 173 miles of track made it the longest railroad in the world at that time. In 1845, Thomson had signed a contract with the Georgia which gave him total control of its routine operations, but Thomson was bored. Unfortunately for him, the company's officers had no inclination of expanding the road further.

The state of Georgia didn't know what it was going to miss when Edgar Thomson decided to pursue his fortune elsewhere. Thomson would have thrived wherever he called home, but had he stayed near the settlement of Thrasherville, it would have been endowed with his knowledge and skill. Thrasherville was just a temporary spot in the evolution of the area from Creek Indian ancestral lands, eventually becoming Atlanta, the hub of the southeastern United States. The Creek ceded their land in this part of Georgia in 1821, and white settlers arrived in 1822. Decatur was founded in 1823, and Whitehall Inn was opened in 1830.

John Thrasher had built a couple of homes and a general store in 1839 near the place where the zero milepost was placed. The milepost marked the spot where the three Georgia railroads would converge when completed. When the planned terminus was moved to its final spot, the settlement was known as Terminus, meaning "the end of the line." By 1842, the settlement of Terminus had six buildings and thirty residents. In 1838, Henry Irby built a tavern and a grocery at a place that was called Buckhead.

A two-story brick railroad depot was built in 1842 at Terminus, and the hamlet's name was changed to Lumpkinville to honor Governor Wilson Lumpkin. Lumpkin asked that the name be changed again, this time to Marthasville for his daughter.

In 1844, a saw mill was built by Jonathan Norcross in Marthasville.

It was the first true manufacturing operation within a hundred miles. Richard Peters, Lemuel Grant, and John Mills, all personal friends of Thomson's, shortly thereafter built a three-story flour mill.

In 1845, Edgar Thomson suggested another name for the hamlet, a name he made up, Atlanta. That title finally stuck. The area exploded with activity and enthusiasm. When the first Georgia Railroad freight and passenger trains arrived from Augusta in September of 1845, the Atlanta Hotel was opened to serve its travelers. Austin Leyden started the village's first foundry and machine shop, The Atlanta Machine Works. From Terminus' thirty residents in 1842, the town grew to over a thousand in 1847 and to twenty-six hundred in 1850. In five more short years, Atlanta would boast six thousand and twenty-five residents.

With Thomson's brains and entrepreneurial skills, the future would have been unlimited to a man like him. The possibility of Thomson's developing the southern and western parts of the state were very real. But, brighter things were in Thomson's future.

Thomson had come to like Georgia; he had a strong affinity for its land, its people and its culture. He wanted to stay in the South, but the only opportunity he had to continue the building of a railroad nearby was in Tennessee. He was guaranteed the position of Chief Engineer of the Nashville & Chattanooga Railroad, but for Thomson the organizers took too long to raise the funds to start it.

Thomson became interested in a project which would connect Philadelphia with Pittsburgh by rail. Thomson was offered the job as the Chief Engineer of the Pennsylvania Railroad. Its backers had organized the company and had raised the funds to get it started before the Nashville & Chattanooga was ready to commence their operations.

Thomson delayed his decision, but then reluctantly accepted the Pennsylvania offer. The knowledge he had acquired in Georgia, usually through his own experiences, served him well in Pennsylvania. He would become the greatest railway executive in the world within a few years.

Thomson would still be involved with the future of Georgia for a few more years. He was obligated by contracts for multiple years with the Georgia Railroad and the Augusta Canal. Always a pragmatist, he began to divest himself of his Georgia properties and stocks, anticipating his departure.

Thomson owned a thousand acres of prime cattle land near the train station at Thomson. He placed an advertisement in the local paper to sell them. Scotsman James Knox and his wife Ruth, newly arrived from upstate New York, were looking for just such an investment, and the sale was completed. With that fine tract of land, in 1845, the Knoxes settled in Thomson with their six-year-old son Charlie, James' two brothers and their wives. The Knox family were hard-working, no-nonsense Christian planters who helped make Thomson a safe and progressive place to raise a family. Charlie and Leila would later have Peter Seymour Knox and his five sisters in that pristine setting. Peter would sire four fine young men, Wyckliffe, Lawrence, Robert, and Peter, who would be active participants in the growth of Thomson and Augusta.

When Thomson undertook the building of a railroad westward from Philadelphia, he moved to one of the hottest economic spots in the country. But as hot as the economy was in Philadelphia, New York, a major rival, was surpassing Philadelphia as far as rail lines were concerned. Thomson would be the man to correct that.

Philadelphia began in 1682, when William Penn established his Quaker colony. Its history was lush; it was the site of the First and Second Continental Congresses, and it was the nation's capital from 1790 - 1800. By 1800, Philadelphia had become one of the country's busiest ports and its largest city with 67,787 residents.

Philadelphia grew into the nation's first major industrial city. But all was not quiet. In response to poor working conditions and unsustainable living wages, in 1835 over 20,000 Philadelphia workers called a general strike for better pay and a ten-hour workday.

Philadelphia was also a great financial center; it was home to the First and Second Banks of the United States and the United States Mint.

Pennsylvania had taken the high road on many public issues, particularly slavery. The state abolished it in 1780 and required any slaves brought to the city to be freed after a six-month residency. During its ten-year stint as the nation's capital, the city exempted members of the legislative branch of the Federal government from this six-month rule, but members of the executive and judicial branches were not exempt, for some strange reason.

President Washington and Vice-President Jefferson brought some of their slaves to Philadelphia as domestic servants. They then evaded the Federal law by shifting their slaves out of the city, bringing in new slaves before the six-month deadline. Finally, Washington replaced his slaves in Philadelphia with German indentured servants.

Indentured servants were men, women, or children who signed a contract, or indenture, to serve their masters, as such, for four to seven years. In return for their future labors, they were paid their passage to America from England and were provided with food, clothing, and shelter during their servitude. It was a great deal if you had a good master.

In the 1840s, immigrants from Ireland and Germany flooded the city. The rich moved west and the immigrants moved into their old houses which had been turned into tenements and boarding houses. Small row houses crowded alleyways and small streets. These areas became filthy with garbage and waste from animal pens piled high. Hundreds died each year from malaria, smallpox, tuberculosis, and cholera caused by poor sanitation and diseases brought in by immigrants.

Many also died from violence. In the 1840s, volunteer fire companies were infiltrated by gangs, and fights between the companies often broke out. At this time, violence against immigrants was common. Workers feared for their jobs; they didn't want the competition and they resented newcomers of different religions and ethnicity, especially the Catholics and the Irish. Violence against blacks was also prevalent. Deadly race riots resulted in the burning of black churches and homes.

In 1841, Joseph Sturge, the English Quaker, wrote that "there is probably no city in this known world where dislike, amounting to the hatred of coloured people, prevails more than in the city of brotherly love." Sturge was an abolitionist and activist who founded the British and the Foreign Anti-Slavery Society. He engaged in radical political actions such as pacifism, working-class rights, and universal emancipation of slaves.

Edgar Thomson agreed with none of Sturge's thoughts. Thomson was a businessman who believed in getting the job done on time and at the least expense. That included manual labor, slave labor, and contract labor. He was anti-union and voiced his concerns about it numerous times.

Thomson was certainly not an abolitionist, and he was certainly not a hater of colored people, free or bonded in chains. Anyone in his time could look at the living conditions of his gandy-dancers and the woodsmen working for him and could see that he was not a great supporter of working-class rights. Neither were the other businessmen of the world, railroaders or not.

Thomson's new baby, his new project, was the Pennsylvania Railroad. Someone had to eliminate the inefficiency of the state-sponsored canals and short-haul railroads. William Williams had gone to Philadelphia to bring Thomson down to Georgia in 1834, and now in 1847, Thomson was reversing that journey.

The Pennsylvania Railroad hired Thomson at a starting salary of $5,000 a year to be its Chief Engineer. The average American worker made less than $500 a year in comparison. Brilliantly, Thomson used grade allowances and river crossings to establish the most efficient and effective routes from Philadelphia to Pittsburgh.

Thomson is most famous in the minds of the few people who know anything about him for constructing the Horseshoe Curve in the Allegheny Mountains of western Pennsylvania in 1854. He is certainly known for it in Pennsylvania. Thomson named the area Alatoona for the Alatoona Gap in Georgia. Pennsylvanians finally dropped the second "a" and renamed it Altoona.

Thomson's co-designer of the Horseshoe Curve was Herman Haupt,

J. EDGAR THOMSON, THE GEORGIA RAIL ROAD YEARS, 1833 – 1845

Abe Lincoln's head of the Transportation Department during the Civil War. Haupt was President Lincoln's second choice; his first choice was Thomson. Thomson didn't want the position due to the time it would take him away from his own railroad and the smaller salary it would pay. Thomson told Lincoln himself to name Haupt as his director, and Lincoln, knowing to whom he was talking, agreed.

Thomson stayed on Lincoln's case during the War, once the Rebels had invaded the North. Thomson was not going to stand by and watch those rednecks wreck the beautiful railroad he had built. All through southern Pennsylvania, Rebels roamed with free will. Thomson had made fast friends with Major General George B. McClellan when McClellan worked as a supervisor on one of Thomson's roads. Thomson personally solicited Abraham Lincoln to form a new Army and to make McClellan the Commander of Thomson's newly proposed Army of Pennsylvania, just to keep the Rebels off his railroads. Lincoln, of course, couldn't stand McClellan's guts, so it was no deal. Thomson hired his own "army" to protect his railroad.

An interesting footnote on the company's books after the War Between the States says that on May 15, 1865, the company's fifteen Negroes were emancipated at a loss of $26,255. These would have included a Negro woman and child William Dearing had purchased. They were the wife and child of a Negro man owned by the railroad. Another of the older Negroes owned by the company applied for a $200 grant to move his family back to Africa, which was given without debate. On the 20th of January, 1864, after Abe Lincoln declared the emancipation of slaves, it was resolved by the Board of Directors that all Negroes traveling on the railroad had to pay full price instead of half fare. The Georgia Railroad had used slave labor from 1840 to 1865.

Thomson not only expanded the company and put it on a strong financial basis, but he also made the railroad the technological leader of the industry. Thomson's road made the first changes from wood to coal, and then from iron to steel. Thomson contracted with his best friend, Andrew

Carnegie, for steel to replace all his wooden railway bridges and to replace all his iron tracks with stronger steel tracks.

Carnegie tried to get Thomson to become a partner with him in building a new steel mill in Braddock, Pennsylvania, very near Pittsburgh. Thomson had as much as he could handle with his railroad and told Carnegie, "Thanks, but no thanks." Carnegie built it on his own; it was called U. S. Steel in later years. Carnegie then offered to have Thomson run it for him, but Thomson declined. To make Thomson feel guilty and accept the offer, Carnegie named the works The Edgar Thomson Steel Works. But Thomson still refused. He told Carnegie, "I told you I was too busy."

Thomson gave most of his business to his friends, his cronies, in Philadelphia. These men were members of his clique, and they had embraced him his whole career. He had started using them while in Georgia with the Baldwin locomotives and had hired the Irish right off the boats in Philadelphia. His clique financed many of Thomson's expansions and projects.

Thomson's organizational model with corporate divisions became the American standard. He also developed a new management style suitable for a large corporation with many functions. He decentralized the old prevailing management system with management based on geographic districts.

Thomson put into place the line and staff system that became the American system of corporate management. Thomson's line executives handled people and hourly decisions on traffic, and his staff executives handled finance and paperwork.

The large-scale problems of management of giant corporations were solved by three railroad engineers: Benjamin Latrobe of the Baltimore and Ohio, Daniel McCallum of the Erie, and Edgar Thomson of the Pennsylvania. Those three engineers, all railroad executives, established functional departments of a corporation. They first defined the lines of authority, responsibility, and communication with a separation of line and staff duties.

Those are the principals of operation and management of the modern American corporation today, patterned from those employed by Thomson. John Edgar Thomson, from Pennsylvania to Georgia and back, spent a lifetime engineering, building, developing, and growing. He could not be derailed. He left a trail of accomplishments.

Epilogue

In addition to Edgar Thomson's position as the first Chief Engineer of the Pennsylvania Railroad, he also became its third President. With 6,000 miles of track, Thomson's Pennsylvania was the largest railroad in the world at that time. Thomson had done for Philadelphia and Pennsylvania what he had done for Augusta and Georgia. The years from 1852 through 1874 when Thomson led the Pennsylvania Railroad were called its "Golden Years."

Thomson made millions through salaries, dividends, and investments, but he never engaged in any negative self-dealings with his companies' stocks. Thomson invested heavily in companies only after he had placed an insider in their operations, but he and his cronies never considered that to be anything other than a normal and prudent business technique in the 1840s through the 1880s.

After the workers' strike in Philadelphia, Thomson's management teams could not regard the company's labor force as just a disposable commodity. Thomson had always paid his laborers in Pennsylvania with the highest of any wages in the industry and provided them with the safest working conditions of any railroad. It was understandable why Thomson was not sympathetic to their demands that they had the right to determine what a fair wage was for their labor.

In 1872, Thomson was forced to recognize the Brotherhood of Locomotive Engineers. The contract stated that wage changes would occur only after consultation with the union representatives. Thomson unilaterally lowered wages by ten percent in 1873, and the engineers in the Midwest struck. Thomson had the state militias called out in Ohio and Indiana, and the strike was quickly broken. Thomson and the bosses of the nation's railroads began to have a foreboding feeling of distrust and fear for the unions and its men.

One feather in the Pennsylvania Railroad's cap was that its growth over so many miles required a coordination of the time all the different railroads left their stations and arrived at the next. In its earlier days, the country had different time schedules because individual postmasters, station masters, and public figures set their local time based on when the sun rose at their locations. The inconsistent time schedules confused passengers from place to place, so the railroad managers reduced their time zones to one hundred from the three hundred being used. That still wasn't good enough. It took until 1883 for the United States to have only four time zones. That was a little better.

In his will, made in December of 1871, Thomson provided for a trust fund which would care for the orphaned daughters of men who had died in the service of his beloved Pennsylvania and Georgia railroads. He purchased the lot next to his home in Philadelphia to build a boarding school for the girls. He wanted to use his home as the orphanage's administration building. But the trust was changed so that Thomson could better support his adopted daughter, who was his wife's niece. The changes were done poorly, exposing the trust to several unexpected liabilities.

The trust was also damaged by a lawsuit in which Thomson had guaranteed $800,000 in some European bonds to get funding for the Pennsylvania. He had exposed his personal assets once again for his beloved railroad. Thomson died on May 27, 1874, and the $800,000 guarantee was still legally enforceable. The estate's lawyers tried to fight it but gave it up as a lost cause. Thomson's estate after paying the guarantee was still worth $1,300,000 in 1874.

The orphanage was delayed until 1882 when the trust purchased two more buildings on Rittenhouse Street. On December 4th, the orphanage's first young ladies entered the J. Edgar Thomson School. Thomson's wife, Lavinia, personally supervised the orphanage until her death.

We have done significant research trying to find more information about the personal lives of J. Edgar Thomson and his wife, Lavinia, but to no avail. The Thomsons were very private people. What we do know is that Lavinia was born on September 17, 1824 and died on November 24, 1903. She was diabetic and died of bronchial pneumonia. Lavinia is buried in Woodlands Cemetery in Philadelphia, next to J. Edgar Thomson.

J. Edgar Thomson never had any children, but held a deep affection for his adopted niece, Miss Charlotte Foster, who had been orphaned at an early age. She lived with the Thomsons after their marriage. Charlotte and Lavinia were both provided with substantial portions of the Thomson estate when he died, before the J. Edgar Thomson Foundation was funded.

Beyond these few tidbits, very little is known of the personal lives of J. Edgar Thomson and his wife, Lavinia.

The school changed its charter in the 1920s. Railway safety procedures had become so well-enforced that the number of girls enrolled dropped to thirty-six. The trustees changed the charter so that orphan girls of railway men who had died natural deaths could be admitted.

In 1923, the trust was amended to allow seventy-five girls to live in their mothers' or guardian's homes. Institutional care was discontinued in 1935. Help in the form of monthly allowances was at that point given to qualified girls from infancy through high school graduation.

The foundation changed once more to allow girls whose fathers or mothers had worked for any railroad to receive monthly stipends. The

John Edgar Thomson Foundation is to this day providing the funds necessary to support those qualified young ladies who need assistance in their education and in their lives. It is a legacy which befits the man.

Acknowledgments

*Grateful acknowledgment is extended to the five brilliant and well-ed-*ucated ladies who proofed this book and offered their timely and excellent advice to me:

Christy Brown
Peggy Lovejoy
Ann Roberts
Lisa Rogers
JoAnn Smith

All rights of ownership to this book have been given to the Thomson—McDuffie Museum. All net revenues from the sale of this book are the property of the Museum, which is located at 121 Main Street, Thomson, GA 30824. It is the best small museum in Georgia. Come see for yourself, or just type in www.mcduffiemuseum.com for its website and reviews.

Bibliography

Arthur, T. (1853) *Lippincott's Cabinet Histories. Georgia*. Philadelphia, PA: Lippincott, Grambo & Co.

Cashin, E. (1995) *Old Springfield, Race and Religion in Augusta, Georgia*. Augusta, GA: The Springfield Village Park Foundation, Inc.

Cashin, E. (1980) *The Story of Augusta*. Augusta, GA: Richmond County Board of Education.

Covington, J. (2008) *Augusta, Georgia, The Canal*. Raleigh, NC: lulu.com.

Cumming, M. (1945) *Georgia Railroad & Banking Company 1833—1945*. Augusta, GA: Walton Printing Company.

Garvey, J. (2000) *Build a Good House*. Augusta, GA: Private Publication.

Green, E. (1936) *George McDuffie*. Columbia, SC: The State Company.

Hillyer, W. (1950) *Cotton and a Yankee Build the Georgia Railroad*. Railroad Magazine.

Krakow, K. (1975) *Georgia Place-Names*. Macon, GA: Winship Press.

Longstreet, A. (1840) *Georgia Scenes, Characters, Incidents, Etc. in the First Half Century of the Republic*. New York, NY: Harper and Brothers.

McCommons, W. and Stovall, C. (2002) *History of McDuffie County, Georgia*. Milledgeville, GA: Boyd Publishing Company.

Milfort, L. (1972) *Memoirs, or a Quick Glance at my Various Travels and my Sojourn in the Creek Nation*. Savannah, GA: Beehive Press.

Mixon, C. (1963) *History of the Georgia Railroad*, an address to the Athens Historical Society. Athens, GA: Unpublished.

Prince, R. (1972) *Steam Locomotives and History: Georgia Railroad and West Point Route*. Salt Lake City, Utah: Wheelwright Lithographing Company.

Sherwood, A. (1970) *A Gazetteer of Georgia*. Atlanta, GA: Cherokee Publishing Company.

Wade, J. (1969) *Augustus Baldwin Longstreet*. Athens, GA: University of Georgia Press.

Ward, J. (1980) *J. Edgar Thomson, Master of the Pennsylvania*. Westport, Conn: Greenwood Press.

Ward, J. (1976) *J. Edgar Thomson and the Georgia Railroad 1834—1847. Railroad History No. 134*. Boston, MA: The Railway and Locomotive Historical Society.

Willingham, R. (2007) *The History of Wilkes County, Georgia*. Washington, GA: Wilkes Publishing Company.

Document No.96, 19th Congress, 2d Session; Message from the President of the United States… in Relation to the Site of the Arsenal of the United States at Augusta, in the State of Georgia. (1826) Washington, D. C.: Gales & Seaton.

Romantic America. (1966) Compiled by Joseph Jobe. Lausanne, Switzerland: Edita.

About the Author

Lewis Smith grew up 150 yards from the main gate of the Augusta National Golf Club. He graduated from Richmond Academy in 1965, attended Georgia Tech for two years and then joined the U. S. Navy. He served on aircraft carriers as a radar/computer specialist on A-6 fighter/bombers. Lewis married a Pittsburgh girl in 1970 and they settled in the Augusta area. Lewis and his wife, JoAnn, started a CPA company and expanded to include the Thomson, Georgia area. They raised two very fine sons there. Both are CPAs today. Jason lives in Augusta and Brian lives in Hawaii. Lewis retired in 2009 when Jason bought his practice. JoAnn worked for Jason until 2016. Lewis became the Director of the Thomson-McDuffie Museum as a volunteer. He spends his time and efforts at the Museum and works in his yard in his spare time. He loves his town, his church, his yard, and his family.

www.ingramcontent.com/pod-product-compliance
Lightning Source LLC
Chambersburg PA
CBHW071732080526
44588CB00013B/1997